Alzheimer's
Activities
That Stimulate
the Mind

Alzheimer's Activities That Stimulate the Mind

Emilia C. Bazan-Salazar, R.N., B.S.N.

McGraw·Hill

New York   Chicago   San Francisco   Lisbon   London   Madrid   Mexico City
Milan   New Delhi   San Juan   Seoul   Singapore   Sydney   Toronto

Library of Congress Cataloging-in-Publication Data

Bazan-Salazar, Emilia C.
 Alzheimer's activities that stimulate the mind / by Emilia Bazan-Salazar.
 —1st ed.
     p.   cm.
   ISBN 0-07-144731-8
   1. Alzheimer's disease—Patients—Rehabilitation.   2. Dementia—Patients—
Rehabilitation.   3. Caregivers.   4. Self-care, Health.   I. Title.

 RC523.B395   2005
 362.196'831—dc22   2004015652

1 2 3 4 5 6 7 8 9 0   DOC/DOC   0 9 8 7 6 5

ISBN 0-07-144731-8

This book is printed on acid-free paper.

Contents

Acknowledgments

I would like to thank my family for their love and support during the writing of this book: my older daughter, Trilina, for her support; my husband, Franklyn, for his technical support; my younger daughter, Natalia, for her art contributions; and my mother, who always raised me to believe in myself.

I would like to thank my agent, Carol von Raesfeld, New Writers Literary Agency, for finding my first book a good home.

Thanks also to the families and the persons living with Alzheimer's who participated in my research, proving that stage-related activities do work.

Introduction

This book was written to introduce you, the caregiver, to areas of activities that produce the maximum mental stimulation necessary for persons living with Alzheimer's disease or dementia as they experience mental decline. *Alzheimer's Activities That Stimulate the Mind* brings together different stage-appropriate activities designed to maintain and enhance the memory and cognitive abilities of persons living with Alzheimer's or dementia (referred to in these pages as "the family member" or "the loved one").

This book is intended to be a guideline so that you can expand on the suggestions and create your own activities suitable to your unique situation. These ideas are appropriate for many levels of care providers—an individual family member taking care of a loved one, a caregiver in a group home or assisted living facility, or a skilled care provider in a full-scale nursing care center.

One of the distinctive qualities of this book is that it provides information regarding what activities are appropriate for each of the specific stages of Alzheimer's. This approach is important in enhancing a person's cognitive abilities with regard to performing activities of daily living (bathing, dressing, shaving, eating, communicating) and also has been proven to help people maintain these abilities much longer than a person who does not participate in stage-appropriate activities.

The individual caregiver has so much to remember—proper diet, doctors' visits, running errands—that the extra time spent caring for a loved one living with Alzheimer's or any other type of dementia can lead to severe role strain. It can become difficult to make time for visiting and having fun. This book will help to relieve the stress of trying to find activities that are right for your loved one. The activities included here are meant to not only enhance the abilities of your loved one but also reduce the strain on you and allow you the opportunity to enjoy the time spent with the person for whom you are caring.

The activities that have been developed for this book are not only proven to maintain and enhance the skills of the person living with Alzheimer's or dementia but also to help dispel the negative stereotype associated with reduced cognitive function. Providing the appropriate stage-related activities enhances both the loved one's and the caregiver's self-esteem. Conversely, attempting to perform activities outside of the person's cognitive ability and skill level reduces self-esteem. It leads to frustration for everyone involved. This frustration can lead to behavior problems and self-isolation for the person living with Alzheimer's or dementia. As each stage of Alzheimer's or dementia develops, a whole new set of problems to overcome develops as well. Providing the right stimulation can make this transition much easier, and reducing the level of frustration enhances the learning process. The goal of these activities is to allow the loved one to keep what he or she has and get back some that has been lost. Naturally, every success will be case-specific, but this book gives both the caregiver and the person living with Alzheimer's or dementia the tools to succeed.

The main concept to remember is to take things slowly—activities should always be performed with a great deal of patience and care. They should be limited to blocks of time between thirty minutes and one hour. We must remember that persons living with Alzheimer's or dementia have different thought processes from those who are not affected, and these thought processes vary with each individual. Activities should be fun; precious moments can be shared between the caregiver and the loved one with the appropriate activities.

Physiological Changes with Aging

In caring for an elderly person or one living with Alzheimer's or dementia, it is often difficult to understand all the terms and explanations used by doctors; however, it is helpful to have a general understanding of what happens as we age. Having a basic familiarity will take some of the fear out of the job of being a caregiver. Even though you may never take someone's blood pressure or interpret a test result, terms such as *hypertension*, *decreased bowel function*, and *osteoporosis* become much less scary when you know how they may apply to the person for whom you are caring. It is much easier and less stressful to perform needed tasks if you know the reasons behind them. It also helps the person living with Alzheimer's to understand the reasons behind some of the changes that are occurring due to advancing age.

It is sometimes easier to remember to apply lotion after a shower, for example, if you, the caregiver, understand that the elderly person's body no longer retains moisture as it used to, or not to put off making that dental appointment because you realize that improperly fitting dentures is the number one cause of malnutrition in elderly people. When performing the activities in this book, it will be a great asset to consider not only the limitations presented by Alzheimer's or dementia but the physiological changes that the person is experiencing as well. Table I.1 outlines some of the frequent changes that occur as a person ages.

So, how does stage-related activity work? It's actually very simple: *stage-related activities enhance cognitive functioning.* Each activity was designed and tested to target specific areas that are lost in each stage of Alzheimer's or other types of dementia. They promote self-esteem by enabling the loved one to succeed and to focus not on the losses the disease produces but on the abilities that the person still has. In many cases, functions thought to be lost are relearned, thereby increasing what the loved one is able to do. The accompanying decrease in frustration leads to happier moods and the ability to be proud of oneself.

Benefits of performing stage-related activities include the following:

- Dispelling the negative stereotype associated with reduced cognitive function of elderly people
- Reinforcing the self-esteem and competence of older people through emphasizing and encouraging their skills and wisdom
- Providing a stimulating and encouraging environment

TABLE I.1 **Physiological Changes**

System/Organ	Change	Result
Cardiovascular	Arterial wall becomes more rigid and cardiac output is reduced.	Traditional methods of measuring blood pressure may not be accurate for persons over age 70; rise in blood pressure (hypertension).
Basal metabolic rate	Basal metabolic rate declines by about 20% between the ages of 20 and 90.	Decrease in activity level.
	The amount of energy expended declines.	A lower caloric intake is needed.
Pulmonary function (lungs)	This function declines by about 40% throughout life.	No restriction in normal activities.
	Air stays in lungs longer, but capacity to take adequate breaths decreases.	May limit the capacity for energetic exercise.
Renal function (kidneys)	Regeneration of *neplocons* (tissues that build up in the kidneys) appears after age 40.	Decreased ability of the kidney to form either a concentrated or a diluted urine.

continued

TABLE I.1 **Physiological Changes** *(continued)*

System/Organ	Change	Result
Renal function (kidneys) *(continued)*	Kidney is in a resting state.	Kidney develops a poor response to stress.
	Glomerular filtration rate declines with age.	Cannot remove impurities from body as before.
	Decrease in renal plasma flow.	Cannot remove impurities from body as before.
Skeletal and muscular system	Due to absorption increase, there is a net loss of bone shown through a thinning of the walls and a decrease in overall skeletal mass.	When loss is severe, the result is osteoporosis (more rapid in women), poor posture, increased curvature of the spine, and shuffling gait.
	Muscle strength and the number of muscle cells decline with age. The muscle mass is replaced with fat tissue.	Loss of strength, and lean body mass decreased.
Gastrointestinal tract (digestion)	Secretion of digestive juices is decreased and less hydrochloric acid is produced. Peptin lipase is also reduced, slowing down the way the body breaks down protein into energy.	Frequent constipation, indigestion; a good mixed diet and exercise can correct these problems.

System/Organ	Change	Result
Dentition	Loss of some or all of the teeth.	Use of dentures, loss of appetite and/or poor eating habits due to inability to chew from lack of dentures or ill-fitting dentures.
	Possible progressive degeneration of tissues around teeth.	Periodontal disease; pain with eating.
Vision	Ability to adapt to dim light declines.	Difficulty distinguishing objects in a poorly lit room.
	Ability to focus at different distances declines.	Presbyopia; can be corrected by lenses
	A yellowing white, opaque ring around the periphery of the iris known as arceis senelis occurs in 40% of older people.	Poor vision, blindness.
	Increased pressure of the aqucous humor.	Glaucoma
	A clouding or opacity of the lens.	Cataracts

continued

TABLE I.1 **Physiological Changes** *(continued)*

System/Organ	Change	Result
Other senses (hearing, taste, smell)	Inability to hear tones of high frequency and distinguish speech patterns from background noise.	Loss of hearing resulting in decreased social interaction (men are more likely to be impaired than women).
	In some areas of the central nervous system, a loss of neurons occurs with age with a concomitant decrease in sensory perceptions.	Loss in number of taste buds and reduced olfactory sensitivity. May result in disinterest in eating.
Endocrine system	Decrease in insulin output by the pancreas.	Diabetes.

- Providing opportunities for learning and practice of cognitive skills in areas that are personally meaningful while still having fun
- Ensuring assessment and treatment of diseases that interfere with maximum cognitive performance
- Providing situations and environments that are conducive to learning

Keep these tips in mind:

- Learning should be interactive.
- Eliminate unnecessary confusion and distraction.

- Multimodal learning using several sensory systems is the most effective. There is some evidence that older adults learn better using auditory—rather than visual—systems. These have been incorporated into the activities in this book.
- Use the principles of cues, practice, and motivation. Don't just do the activity for the loved one; offer guidance and provide help when necessary. Independence is the goal.

What Is Dementia?

What does the term *dementia* mean? Is it the same for everyone? How long does it last? These are some very common and frightening questions. There are many types of dementia—Alzheimer's is just one of them. Dementia itself is neither a disease nor a diagnosis but a "syndrome," which is a descriptive term for a "collection of symptoms."

The cognitive deterioration associated with dementia is acquired later in life, not present from birth as in mental retardation. The symptoms of dementia are primarily behavioral, not physical. These changes in behavior are:

- not part of normal aging
- not irreversible—10 percent to 20 percent of the causes of dementia are treatable (e.g., caused by depression, thyroid imbalance, participating in the wrong activities, etc.)
- not universal—not every person with dementia has every symptom

- not unilateral—for a particular individual, some symptoms may be severe and others barely noticeable
- not consistent—at one time of the day or week, the symptoms may be present, and at other times, they may not

Dementia is defined as a decline in intellectual function marked by a global cognitive impairment (i.e., memory impairment) and at least one of the following:

- Impairment of abstract thinking
- Impairment of judgment
- Impairment of other complex capabilities such as language use, ability to perform complex physical tasks, ability to recognize objects or people, or ability to construct objects
- Personality changes

Disorders That Cause Dementia

The following is a partial list of the potentially reversible causes of dementia or dementia-like behavior:

- Acute physical illness
- Alcoholism
- Brain tumor
- Chemical intoxication
- Depression
- Drug toxicity
- Electrolyte imbalance
- Hormone imbalance

- Hypothermia
- Hypothyroidism or hyperthyroidism
- Infections of the central nervous system
- Liver or kidney dysfunction
- Metabolic imbalance
- Normal pressure hydrocephalus (pressure caused by fluids built up around the brain)
- Pernicious anemia
- Psychotic state
- Sensory deprivation
- Sensory losses (e.g., vision and hearing)
- Vitamin deficiency

Alzheimer's disease is the most common form of dementia. AD alone accounts for 50 percent of cases of dementia. Another 20 percent of cases have a combination of AD and multi-infarct dementia (stroke).

What Is Alzheimer's Disease?

Alzheimer's disease (AD) is a progressive neurological disease characterized by the following pathological changes in the brain, which are greater than those associated with normal aging:

- **Neurofibrilla tangles.** These are the many tiny fibrils that extend in every direction from the nerve body, which relay and deliver messages from the brain. In normal aging, they sometimes become tangled and prevent the correct message from being either delivered or received.

■ **Senile plaques.** These are patches of brain tissue that become hardened and no longer have the capabilities to relay messages.

■ **Brain atrophy.** This is when the brain tissue itself wastes or decreases in size, which diminishes the brain's capacity to relay messages.

These brain changes can be absolutely identified only by an autopsy. Consequently, the diagnosis of AD in a living patient is a clinical one, based on a detailed history, current behavioral symptoms, and exclusion of all other possible causes of these symptoms. AD is a neurological disease, but the primary symptoms, particularly in the early and middle stages, are behavioral, not physical.

The progression of AD is variable, with the course running anywhere from three to twenty years from the first symptoms until death. The average course is seven or eight years, characterized by a progressive decline.

Stage Categories

The following overview will help you gauge the appropriate activity level for your loved one. The activities have been designed to maintain and help prevent further loss of skills that are specific to each stage.

■ **Stage One:** These persons are considered in the early stages of Alzheimer's disease. There is some memory loss, which is periodic and inconsistent and occurs particularly in new surroundings. These persons are still able to perform many or all of the activities of daily living (ADLs), such as bathing and dressing, feeding themselves, and doing light housekeeping. They are able to communicate their needs and understand what others are saying to them. At this stage they are somewhat forgetful and may have the beginnings of low self-esteem related to their forgetfulness. Many people at this stage attribute their forgetfulness to lack of sleep or too much stress, both of which can cause the symptoms.

- **Stage Two:** These persons are in the middle stages of AD and demonstrate the same type of memory loss as Stage One but are less able to dress themselves, feed themselves, or perform daily hygiene. They will sometimes mismatch clothing or forget to bathe or shave. They may need cueing or directions from the caregiver. They will often become agitated when reminded, and there is an increase in memory loss. They will require more supervision at this point. Meals, bill paying, and major decisions usually become the responsibility of the caregiver; however, the loved one may still be able to have some input. Self-isolation may become a problem in Stage Two as the person understands the need for additional help. Activities will play an important part in rebuilding self-esteem and maintaining skills.

- **Stage Three:** These persons are considered in the advanced stages of Alzheimer's or dementia. Verbal cues are not enough at this point, and constant supervision is needed. Language skills may show signs of decline and may have deteriorated to the point that only simple phrases or familiar expressions persist. They may not be able to communicate their needs clearly or to understand what is being said to them, and they will often become agitated because of their confusion. They will need to be dressed and have their food set up for them. Bathing and shaving will become the responsibility of the caregiver. Incontinence, both fecal and urinary, is common in this stage. The ability to perform ADLs varies greatly depending on the individual. Usually, the person being cared for will no longer be able to perform activities such as grocery shopping, bill paying, and decision making. They may still be able to walk and feed themselves, but other activities will have to be performed for them to varying degrees. For someone living with the loss of skills that most people take for granted, activities that the person can perform successfully help to rebuild self-esteem and maintain skills. For the caregiver, engaging in the activities provides an opportunity to take a break and enjoy the time together.

- **Stage Four:** These persons are in the end stage and are completely dependent on the caregiver to meet all their needs. There could be a complete loss of language capabilities at this time. The patient may be unable to move, speak, or swallow. The caregiver and the person being cared for need quality time outside of the daily care regimen, which can be hectic and often seem impossible to maintain. Activities at this point will provide time for joy and laughter. Sometimes that little bit of time out that you both can simply enjoy will get you through the day with a smile.

Each activity in the following chapters lists the stage or stages for which it was designed and the skills that it will maintain and enhance. Use these guidelines to match the appropriate activity with your loved one's skill level.

Alzheimer's Activities That Stimulate the Mind

Arts and Crafts

Crafts are an important tool in increasing satisfaction in all types of settings. Crafts provide a method of expression for creative energy as well as a simple way to experience pleasure in doing. Successful completion of a craft item can foster feelings of personal accomplishment, and the product can be easily displayed and admired. Craft items can be useful in many ways, allowing the creators to feel that their efforts have significant purpose. This goes a long way in boosting all-important self-esteem.

Ideas

Besides being fun to do, craft activities offer many therapeutic benefits:

1

- Crafts are great gift items for family and friends.
- Crafts can be sold or donated to the neighborhood bazaar.
- Crafts can be a useful service project if items are donated to an organization such as an orphanage, a children's hospital, or a facility for people with disabilities.
- Crafts can be used to decorate rooms.
- A craft item is a tangible object to show and discuss with visitors.
- The skills involved can be taught to others.

Adaptations can be made in crafts projects to enable participation by people with functional limitations. For instance, people with visual handicaps can use oversize knitting needles and crochet hooks with heavy yarn, or projects can be done assembly-line fashion, with the caregiver working on the overall project and others doing the portions that they can manage best. However, a word of caution: *Do not make the craft for the individual for whom you are caring.* The primary value of the craft is the satisfaction the person receives from doing and accomplishing. Better the slightly imperfect piece that a person can display as his or her own, than the more polished item made by someone else.

Here are some tips to help ensure success:

- Know basic crafts (as discussed in this chapter).
- Know where to get materials.
- Know how to prepare materials and equipment.
- Know how to use necessary equipment.
- Do not insist on perfection.
- Be able to help at any stage of a project.

- Provide some means of utilization of the person's finished projects, such as putting them on display or giving them to friends, relatives, or organizations.
- Know variations of crafts procedures in order to keep the person's interest and to offer varied opportunities depending on the person's level of ability.
- Use safety precautions such as proper lighting, correct use of knives and scissors, and nontoxic materials for people with allergies.
- Know where to look for immediate assistance—books, pamphlets, other people, and the Internet are often useful resources.
- Before beginning any project, assemble all necessary equipment in your chosen work area.

Purchasing supplies through arts and crafts stores can be expensive. You can save money by purchasing many of the basic supplies and ingredients in the following list at your local supermarket. The formulas are easy to prepare and can be mixed in advance and stored for future use in order to enhance the quality time spent on an activity.

Any activity that the person you are caring for used to perform can be incorporated into your activity planning. Many of the recipes presented in the following section do not have corresponding activities within this book. They have been provided to meet your creative needs. Remember to always monitor the making of these products and provide hands-on help as needed.

Formulas and Hints

Candle Wax

Wax from old candles is best. Paraffin is also good, but it melts rapidly. Beeswax also is excellent but is more expensive. Mutton tallow makes wonderful hard candles, but it becomes rancid. Here are two formulas that work well:

- 60% by weight paraffin
- 35% stearic acid
- 5% beeswax

or

- 10 ounces mutton tallow
- 4 ounces beeswax
- 2 ounces alum
- ½ ounce gum camphor

Fixative

Fixatives are liquid mixtures used to "fix" chalk and charcoal work so that the image will not smear or rub off. The mixture is sprayed through an insect sprayer or atomizer. You can make any amount that is needed by following the recipe below:

- 6 parts methyl alcohol (rubbing alcohol)
- 1 part shellac
- 1 part paste

Methyl alcohol can be purchased at any arts and crafts store or neighborhood drugstore. Use clear shellacking paste, also found at the arts and crafts store.

Glossy Plaster Finish

Dissolve white soap flakes in enough water to make it the consistency of thin cream, usually two parts water, one part soap flakes. Soak the plaster cast or carving thoroughly in the solution for at least thirty minutes. Remove and polish with a dry cloth.

Paint Containers

Plastic milk cartons with the tops removed make sturdy and stable containers for water and paint. All leftovers should be discarded. Wash out the cartons with soap and water and store for further use.

Paint Dispensers

Plastic mustard or ketchup containers make good paint dispensers. An aluminum nail in the top of each will keep the paint fresh. Syrup pitchers also make good paint dispensers. Keep plastic spoons in cans of powdered tempera for easy dispensing.

Parchment Paper

Brush the surface of a piece of cream-colored manila paper with burnt linseed oil; brush the back of the paper with turpentine and allow to dry.

Heat the linseed oil to just before boiling, then let it cool to room temperature. Place the paper you are preparing on a piece of waxed paper about one inch larger around all sides of the paper. You will need two soft boar bristle brushes. Use a small amount (you do not want it to drip) on the brush and lightly coat the front of the paper with the prepared linseed oil. Turn the paper over, keeping it on the waxed paper, and using a clean brush, coat the back of the paper with turpentine. Again, use only a small amount. Allow to dry at least twenty-four hours before using.

Clean both brushes with turpentine and wipe dry with a paper towel after using.

Note: If you have any problem with the paper curling, cover the paper with another piece of waxed paper and place a book or paperweight on top until dry.

Plaster

Pour a small amount of water into a bowl or pan. Sift handfuls of plaster of paris through your fingers into the water until the plaster builds up above the surface of the water. Now mix it well with your hands. Once the plaster has been mixed, powder or water cannot be added; a separate batch must be made. Caution: Do not mix until all of the powder is sifted into the water. Clean up all plaster before it hardens. Do not pour plaster down a sink or drain. Make sure to clean your hands outside with soap and water to prevent the plaster from hardening in the drain.

Plastic Foam

- 6 tablespoons plastic starch
- 1 cup powdered detergent
- Powdered color for tinting (optional)

The best product to use for powdered color is dry tempera paint. Slowly add water (approximately ½ cup) until moist, whipping continuously with an eggbeater until it reaches the consistency of marshmallow cream (about two to five minutes).

Salt and Cornstarch Clay

- 1 cup salt
- ½ cup cornstarch
- ¼ cup water

Heat ingredients in a double boiler, stirring occasionally with a wooden spoon, until mixture comes to a full boil.

Continue to stir for about two minutes over medium heat until mixture forms a globlike mass. Place the mass on waxed paper until it is cool enough to handle: then knead (like bread dough) for three minutes for a firm bread-dough consistency.

The clay can then be wrapped in aluminum foil and stored in the refrigerator for further use. Allow clay to return to room temperature before using. It will keep for up to seven days but must be kneaded again before each use. The clay works well around wires or armatures.

Salt and Flour Clay

- 1 cup salt
- 1 cup flour
- 1 tablespoon alum

Slowly add enough water, stirring constantly with a wooden spoon, until it reaches the consistency of putty.

Salt and Flour Gesso

- 2 cups flour
- 1 cup salt
- 1½ to 2 cups water

Mix until paste is smooth and does not stick to the fingers. Gesso can be used for many activities, such as raised painting projects or finger painting.

Canned Milk Gesso

- 1 part powdered white tempera paint
- 1 part canned milk

Mix and brush on.

Salt and Flour Mixture

- ⅔ cup table salt
- ½ cup water
- ½ cup flour
- 2 or 3 drops food coloring (optional)
- A few drops of oil of clove (optional)—adds a pleasant aroma

Heat the salt in a small frying pan over low heat until it starts making a snapping sound, then pour it into a bowl. Add flour, then water, and mix. Knead dough until it does not stick. Add coloring and clove oil: continue to knead until the color is evenly distributed.

Salt and Flour Relief Mixture

- 3 parts salt
- 1 part flour

Mix with water for desired consistency.

Salt Beads

- 2 parts salt
- 1 part flour
- Water

Mix ingredients, slowly adding water, to reach a doughlike consistency. If color is desired, add dry pigment or food coloring. Break off small pieces and form into beads. Pierce each with a toothpick and allow it to dry; then string.

Sawdust and Wheat Paste for Modeling

- 1 part wheat paste
- 2 parts sawdust
- 1 part water (added one tablespoon at a time)

Slowly add warm water, stirring constantly, to form a smooth and creamy mixture. Add sawdust and mix until paste becomes like putty, approximately two minutes. You may add more water if the mixture becomes too hard or dry.

Simulated Marble

- 2 parts vermiculite
- 2 parts modeling clay
- 1 part water (added one tablespoon at a time)

Combine dry ingredients and slowly add water, stirring constantly until the mixture becomes creamy. Line a medium-size cardboard box with waxed paper. Pour mixture into box and allow it to harden. Model with knife, rasp, sandpaper, or similar tool.

Simulated Stone

- 1 part sand
- 1 part cement
- 4 parts Zonalite
- 1 part modeling plaster

or

- 2 parts sand
- 2 parts cement
- 4 parts Zonalite

Use any fast-drying cement, which can be found at your local hardware store. Zonalite is lightweight foam cement that can be purchased at any arts and crafts store. Combine ingredients, and slowly add enough water to form a thick paste. The amount of water will depend on your project, but it is usually one to two parts. Pour into an unlined cardboard box or mold and allow to harden overnight before removing.

Soda and Cornstarch Clay

- 1 cup cornstarch
- 2 cups baking soda
- 1 ¼ cups water

Combine ingredients and cook over medium heat, stirring constantly, until mixture reaches a doughlike consistency. Turn out onto a piece of aluminum foil or breadboard. Food coloring may be worked into the clay when it has cooled slightly. Clay may be rolled and cut into shapes or modeled. Wrap clay with aluminum foil or place in a plastic bag to keep it pliable when not in use.

Stencil Paper

Melt two to four ounces of paraffin in a large, shallow pan over very low heat. Holding the end of a sheet of typing paper with tweezers or tongs, run the paper through the melted paraffin. Allow the paraffin to set by holding the paper over the pan for just a short time. Recoat the paper in the same manner and allow it to dry by hanging it up with lightweight clamps or by laying it on waxed paper. Stencil paper is now ready to be used.

Synthetic Oil Paint

Add dry color to regular wheat paste that has been mixed to a thin, smooth consistency. Apply with a stiff brush.

Tempera Paint for Glossy Surfaces

Liquid detergent or a few drops of glycerin mixed with tempera paint enables the paint to adhere to shiny or oily surfaces such as aluminum foil and glass.

Translucent Paper

To make paper translucent, brush or wipe on a mixture of 2 parts turpentine and 1 part linseed oil and allow it to dry.

Transparent Paper

Applying 2 parts linseed oil and 1 part turpentine to the back of a drawing with a brush or rag will cause the illustration to become transparent.

Zonalite Sculpture Cement

- 1 part cement
- 1 part Zonalite
- 1 to 2 parts water

Mix cement and Zonalite with water until smooth. Pour into cardboard box or mold to harden. Zonalite cement is lightweight and can be cut with a saw or carved with any metal tool.

Cleaners and Thinners

Now that we're done, how do we clean up the mess? Table 1.1 lists some helpful cleanup tips you will want to keep on hand for these and other activities you might have. Remember that some of the chemicals may be toxic and should be kept locked away when not in use. *Never leave the person in your care unsupervised with any of the chemicals.*

TABLE 1.1. **Cleaners and Thinners**

Medium	Thinner	Cleaner
Shellac	Alcohol	Alcohol
Oil paint	Turpentine or linseed oil	Turpentine and soap or detergent
Enamel	Turpentine	Turpentine
Lacquer	Lacquer thinner	Lacquer thinner
Printer's ink	Printer's varnish	Carbon tetrachloride
Textile paint	Thinner	Cleaner
Any water-based paint, including water color, tempera, showcard, India ink, finger paint, Kemtone, Texalite	Water	Water
Rubber cement	Rubber cement thinner or benzine	Eraser

Antiqued Flowers

Stages: One and Two

Location: Outdoors or inside with adequate ventilation

Equipment: Plastic flowers—used or new; newspaper; one-half pint varnish; one pint turpentine; one ounce powdered gold (treasure gold); half-inch paintbrush; block of Styrofoam

Description of Activity

- Clean plastic flowers, if necessary, and let them dry thoroughly.
- Cover the work area with newspaper.
- Mix the varnish and turpentine together, and stir in the powdered gold.
- Paint the flowers and leaves with the liquid mixture, and then stick the stems into the Styrofoam so the flowers can dry without touching.
- Clean the brush and work area immediately in turpentine.
- Arrange dry flowers in decorative containers.

Goals: Create a simple, attractive gift or room decoration that can make use of discarded plastic flowers; maintain and improve hand-eye coordination; build self-esteem

Adaptation: For an attractive container, make a vase out of any suitable item using Tissue Paper Collage (see page 49).

Asian Beanbags

Stages: One through Three

Location: Inside

Equipment: Scraps of contrasting fabric; ruler; scissors; sewing machine or needle and thread; small dried beans or rice

Description of Activity

■ Following the accompanying diagram, for each beanbag, cut four pieces of contrasting fabric into strips one and three-quarters inches by four and a half inches.

■ Using a quarter-inch seam allowance, sew two strips together into an L shape. Do the same with two more strips, but make a reversed L shape.

■ Sew the two L shapes together, keeping the colors opposite, such as blue to white and white to blue.

ASIAN BEANBAGS

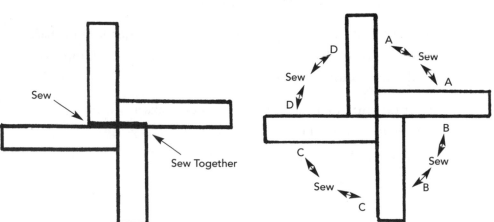

- Sew all four strips together along the long sides. Sew the remaining tops together, but leave one end open.
- Fill with rice or beans and sew closed.
- Make about ten of these for the jacks game (see Adaptation).

Goals: Sense of accomplishment; maintain and improve hand-eye coordination; ease manipulation with arthritic hands

Adaptation: Play a game of "Asian Jacks" using the beanbags instead of jacks—throw up one bag, pick up one; throw up one bag, pick up two; continue until all ten beanbags have been picked up. Makes a worthwhile gift for children. Dimensions in the diagram can be adapted to suit your needs. Be creative with the colors.

Bird Feeder

Stages: One through Four

Location: Inside or outdoors

Equipment: One-pound metal can such as a coffee can; can opener; two plastic lids that fit the can; scissors; dowel or straight stick nine to ten inches long; enamel paint and brushes; wire pants hanger; birdseed

Description of Activity
- Open both ends of a coffee can with a can opener.
- Place a plastic lid on each end of the can, making sure the fit is snug.

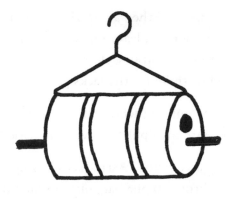

BIRD FEEDER

- In each plastic top, cut a one-and-a-half-inch hole with a pair of scissors. The holes should line up at either end. This creates the bird entrance.

- In the same way, cut a smaller hole in each lid approximately one inch below the bird entrance. Insert the dowel or stick through these holes to make the perch. If the dowel is too long, it may be cut with a small handsaw.

- When you are ready to decorate the bird feeder, remove the plastic lids and use enamel paints. Snap on the lids after paint is completely dry.

- Now remove the cardboard bar from the pants hanger. Bend the hanger down so that the two ends, which held the cardboard bar, will act as hooks to hold up the coffee can. Pierce the uppermost part of the plastic lid with scissors and work each end of the hanger through the lid until secure.

- Fill the feeder by covering one end of the bird feeder and slowly pouring birdseed through the other end. Use just enough seed so that it will not cover the perch. (You will need to empty the feeder of discarded seed hulls prior to each refilling.)

■ Hang the feeder outside in an area best suited for watching birds.

Goals: Pleasure in making something everyone can enjoy; involve family members in project; maintain and increase hand-eye coordination and certain restorative skills (color recognition; function of bird feeder)

Adaptation: The design and decorations are limited only by one's imagination. For example, this project can be combined with a paper collage project, or silk flowers can be glued to the can. It's nice to let the loved one choose what to do and see what happens. The finished product will be a joy to both the caregiver and the loved one who participates in its creation, as well as family members and others who receive the pleasure of watching the birds.

Birdhouse

Stages: One and Two

Location: Inside or outdoors

Equipment: Plywood; square; pencil; saws; hammer; half-inch nails; sandpaper; paint and brushes

Description of Activity:
■ Adapt the accompanying patterns to fit the size of birdhouse desired. You will need five rectangle pieces, two squares, and two triangles.
■ Trace patterns onto the wood and cut out the pieces with a saw.

■ Assemble the ends, roof, floor, and perch and nail the pieces together.

■ Sand until all surfaces are smooth.

■ Paint any color desired.

■ Place near a window, in a tree, or on a stand in an area best suited for watching birds.

Goals: Mental relaxation; identification of birds provides mental stimulation

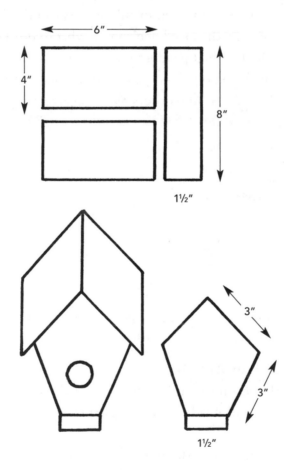

BIRDHOUSE

Adaptation: Family members may wish to provide bread crumbs or birdseed or a birdbath near the birdhouse to attract more birds. Stage Three and Four individuals may enjoy watching and feeding the birds. They can also help paint the finished product.

Bulletin Board

Stages: One through Three

Location: Inside or outdoors

Equipment: Heavy fabric, such as burlap or rice sack; scissors; heavy cardboard, corkboard, or Styrofoam; taper; kraft paper or heavy wrapping paper; glue or rubber cement; rickrack or felt; adhesive picture hanger

Description of Activity
- Cut the fabric about one and a half inches larger on all sides than the board.
- Spread the board with glue and cover it with the fabric.
- Fold the edges under and tape them to the back of the board. (Don't use glue at this point because it will not hold.)
- Cut the kraft paper to fit the board and glue it to the back side to cover the raw edges of the fabric.
- Glue rickrack or felt designs around the border on the front of the board for trim.
- Attach the adhesive hanger at top center on the back side.

Goals: In addition to creating an attractive decoration for any room to display information or pictures, as the loved one's memory begins to fail, the bulletin board will serve as a focal point for reminders about everyday appointments, to-do lists, and—as the Alzheimer's progresses—pictures of family members with their names.

Adaptation: The bulletin board also makes a good bazaar item. Decorations and trim can be of various designs and colors. Painted thumbtacks may be used to hold attachments; however, map tacks may be easier to handle.

Button Pictures

Stages: One through Three

Location: Inside or outdoors

Equipment: Variety of buttons; fabric; strong needle and thread or glue

Description of Activity
- Arrange buttons on a piece of fabric in any design, such as an animal, a flower, or the person's initials. Use buttons of many sizes, colors, and shapes.
- Glue or stitch the buttons into place.

Goals: Outlet for creativity and self-expression; maintain and improve hand-eye coordination

Adaptation: This can be an amusing and entertaining group project involving all members of the family. It could be used to make a pillow.

Clothespin Horse

Stages: One through Three

Location: Inside

Equipment/Supplies: Three old-fashioned clothespins (without springs); thin wire; empty wooden thread spool; scissors; small pieces of felt, any color; glue; short pieces of yarn; colored felt-tip pen.

Description of Activity

▪ Clothespins come with a ball at one end and two prongs, which are used to pin the clothing to the line. Take two clothespins and put the ball ends together with the prongs facing in opposite directions. One end will be the ears of the horse and the other end will form the front legs.

▪ Holding the ball ends together, wrap the wire around both balls to secure.

▪ Place the wooden spool next to the front legs and run the wire through the center of the spool of thread. Pull it taut. This forms the body of the horse.

▪ Place the third clothespin, prongs facing down, at the end of the spool to form the back legs. Wrap the remaining wire around the ball portion of the third clothespin and secure by tucking the wire back through the spool.

▪ Cut out a small circle of felt, then cut two small slits just large enough for the front prongs (ears) to fit through. Slide it over the prongs to form the hat.

▪ Cut out a rectangle piece of felt and glue it to the rounded part of the spool (what is now the horse's back). This forms the blanket of the horse.

CLOTHESPIN HORSE

- Glue strands of yarn on the back clothespin to form a tail.
- Use a felt-tip colored pen to draw the eyes, mouth, and nose.

Goals: Give a sense of accomplishment and the pleasure of making something unique; improve and maintain hand-eye coordination, and maintain color recognition skills

Adaptation: Without the hat and blanket, this could be a reindeer and used as a Christmas decoration: brown pipe cleaners can be used to form antlers, and a small piece of red felt can be used for the nose. Great bazaar items or gifts for grandchildren.

Decorative Pin

Stages: One and Two (Three and Four with hand-over-hand assistance)

Location: Inside or outdoors

Equipment: Clear contact paper; scissors; colorful stamp, small photograph, or similar image; pin clasp backing; glue

Description of Activity

- Cut two pieces of contact paper at least one inch bigger than the stamp or other image—a half-inch border should suffice.
- Remove the backing from the contact paper and place both pieces on the table, sticky side up. Place the back of the stamp in the center of one piece of contact paper. Stick the other piece of contact paper on top of the stamp. Press out all of the air bubbles. Trim around the sides.
- Glue the pin clasp to the back of the stamp, or affix it with a small piece of contact paper.

Goals: Maintain and improve hand-eye coordination; experience success and ability to wear object immediately

Adaptation: Clear contact paper can enclose any number of items—pictures and mementos, cards, and so forth. Large pieces of contact paper can be used to make place mats that are easily washable. Different place mats could be made for each holiday and reused year after year.

Dried Flowers

Stages: One and Two; Three with hand-over-hand assistance

Location: Inside, in-room, or outdoors

Equipment: Fresh flowers; scissors; florist's wire; borax; plastic bag; wire tie; six-by-six-inch cardboard box; florist's tape

Description of Activity

- Gather fresh flowers just prior to full bloom. Remove stems.
- For each flower, cut a length of florist's wire twice the desired length of stem.
- Insert the wire through the base of the flower (where the flower meets the stem), and twist the ends together to form a stem.
- Pour about an inch of borax into the bottom of a plastic bag and place several flowers facedown in the borax. Add more borax to cover the flowers. Continue layering borax and flowers until bag is almost full. (Monitor the activity to assure no one eats the borax.)
- Gather the top of the bag, squeezing out air, and secure it with a tie. Wire stems are sticking out of the bag.
- Place bag in cardboard box and store in dry place for about a month.
- At end of month, remove flowers from bags, carefully blowing or brushing away borax.
- Wrap stems with florist's tape and arrange in vase.

Goals: Creation of a simple craft project that can be fun and decorative and does not require a great deal of skill or coordination

Adaptation: Dried flowers can be used in small bunches to decorate a wreath (see "Pinecone Wreath" in this chapter), or you can make an entire wreath of dried flowers by attaching the flowers to a Styrofoam form with florist's picks.

Eye of God

Stages: One through Three

Location: Inside or outdoors

Equipment: Two eighteen-inch dowels; small handsaw; measuring tape; yarn

Description of Activity

■ Cut a V-shaped slot at the middle of each dowel. Use measuring tape to ensure you are at the center of the dowel. Place a small amount of glue in each slot, and put slots together to form a crossbar. Let the crossbar dry overnight.

■ When the glue is dry, secure the end of the yarn to the center of the crossbar and loop the yarn at least four times around the center of the crossbar. It should look like an X, which will secure the glued area of the crossbar.

■ Next, while turning the crossbar clockwise, loop the yarn around each dowel, pull tight, and then stretch the yarn to the next dowel. Repeat this process until the end of the dowels have been reached.

■ Secure the end of yarn by tying a knot and dabbing a bit of the glue on it. Once dry the Eye of God may be suspended from a piece of string or attached to the wall.

Adaptation: Any color yarn or combination of colors may be used. Simply tie the ends of different colors of yarn together and trim ends when changing colors or adding more yarn. It makes great holiday gifts.

Greeting Card Holder

Stages: One through Three

Location: Inside or outdoors

Equipment: Large juice can; ball of yarn—stretch yarn works best; glue; scissors

Description of Activity
- Wash can and remove both ends.
- Glue end of yarn to inside of can.
- Wrap yarn from top to bottom around the can, covering the openings, until the can is completely covered.
- Glue the free end of the yarn to the inside of the can.
- Insert greeting cards under individual strands, aligning the spines of the cards with the yarn.

Goals: Sense of satisfaction and pleasure in making something attractive and useful; maintain and improve hand-eye coordination and restorative skills

Adaptation: Use red or green yarn for displaying Christmas cards.

Holiday Mobile

Stages: One through Four

Location: Inside

Equipment: Holiday-specific patterns such as hearts, shamrocks, or pumpkins; colored construction paper; aluminum foil; scissors; cardboard; stapler; plastic curtain ring; thread; crepe paper; glue

Description of Activity

- Cut desired designs from the construction paper and/or foil.
- Cut cardboard into a strip one inch wide and eighteen inches long. Form the strip into a circle and staple the ends together.
- Suspend the cardboard circle horizontally from the curtain ring with nine-inch threads.
- Cut crepe paper streamers of varying lengths and glue them to the cardboard.
- Glue the holiday designs and patterns here and there to the streamers.

Goals: Opportunity to involve everyone in a holiday celebration; outlet for creativity; maintain and improve restorative skills and fine motor coordination

Adaptation: Simply by changing the color scheme you can adapt this activity for any occasion.

- Pink and white streamers with red hearts for Valentine's Day
- Green and white streamers with shamrocks for St. Patrick's Day
- Pastel streamers with colored eggs and bunnies for Easter

- Red, white, and blue streamers with silver foil stars for the Fourth of July
- Orange and black streamers with ghosts, black cats, and pumpkins for Halloween
- Red and green streamers with bells, candy canes, trees, stars, snowmen, wreaths, globe-shaped ornaments, and snowflakes for Christmas
- Silver, black, and gold streamers with year numbers, champagne flutes, hats, and noisemakers for New Year's

Marble Painting

Stages: One through Four

Location: Inside or outdoors

Equipment: Plastic half-gallon or one-gallon ice cream pail; construction paper; pencil; scissors; poster paints; four or five marbles; a painter's bib

Description of Activity

- Place the pail on the construction paper and trace around the bottom. Cut out the circle and place it in the bottom of the pail.
- Place several drops of paint of various colors on the paper circle. Drop marbles into the pail and roll them around. Marbles will create the painting. If you want more color, add more paint.
- Make a collage of finished paintings. Shapes such as stars, bells, and trees (depending on the holiday) can be cut out and glued onto construction paper.

Goals: Increase self-esteem and provide a meaningful activity; also another great way of involving any children in the home, which will increase socialization skills

Miniature Tetherball Set

Stages: One and Two

Location: Inside or outdoors

Equipment: Twelve-by-twelve-inch plywood board; fourteen-by-fourteen-inch piece of canvas; ruler; pencil; size 9 penny nail; twelve-inch dowel, a half-inch in diameter; twelve-inch piece of string; large needle; one-inch-diameter Styrofoam ball; small handsaw; glue; staple gun with half-inch staples

Description of Activity

■ First glue the piece of canvas to the plywood board and secure the bottom with staples.

■ Find the center of the board and mark it on the top and bottom of the board with a pencil. You can find the center by measuring six inches from all sides.

■ Align the dowel with the center mark on the canvas-covered side.

■ From the underside of the board, drive a nail through the board at the center mark, attaching the dowel to the other side of the board.

■ Make a quarter-inch slit at the top of the dowel with a small handsaw.

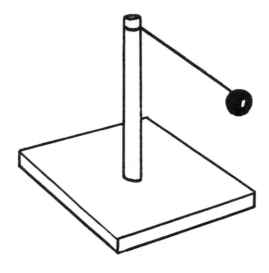

MINIATURE TETHERBALL

■ Slide one end of the string through the slit at the top of the dowel and tie the string around the top portion of the pole. Dab a bit of glue to the top of the dowel and around the dowel where the string is tied to secure it. Allow eight inches to hang loose.

■ Thread the string through the eye of the needle, and run the string through the foam ball. Tie a knot at the end and dab a bit of glue on either end of the ball to secure the string.

How to Play: Tetherball can be played solo or with other players by swatting the tetherball around the pole with your hands. Set a time limit of ten or fifteen minutes. Each player gets one point for wrapping the ball completely around the pole. The opponent attempts to swat the ball back to prevent it from wrapping around the pole. If playing solo, the goal is to wrap the ball completely around the pole with one swat.

Patchwork Place Mat

Stages: One and Two (Three and Four with adaptation)

Location: Inside

Equipment: Cardboard; ruler; pencil; scissors; fabric scraps; needle and thread; sewing machine (optional)

Description of Activity

- Cut a four-inch square out of the cardboard. Use the cardboard square as a pattern to cut squares from the fabric scraps. You'll need twelve fabric squares for each place mat—three down and four across.

- Sew the fabric squares together with needle and thread; seam allowance should be small, approximately a quarter inch, so the squares will not be too bulky. If desired, squares may again be stitched on the sewing machine for durability. (For stages Three and Four, the squares can be glued to the cardboard using any brand of white glue. Squeeze a small amount of glue onto the four-inch piece of cardboard, and spread with fingers or paintbrush. Apply the fabric to this and allow to dry for at least an hour before continuing.)

- Cut a rectangle twelve by sixteen inches from a solid piece of scrap fabric for the lining. Sew wrong sides of the patchwork and lining together, either by hand or by machine, leaving an opening large enough to turn the place mat right side out.

- Turn the place mat right side out, and whipstitch the opening closed. If you're using a sewing machine, the entire place mat can now be topstitched around the outer edge.

Goals: Simple, repetitive tasks, which can easily be performed assembly-line fashion with persons in lower-level stages

Adaptation: These same patchwork squares can be made into pillow tops, lap rugs, coverlets, and other articles. Makes a unique wedding gift.

Photo Mobile

Stages: One and Two (Three and Four with assistance)

Location: Inside

Equipment: Two twelve-inch dowels; glue; wire; scissors; construction paper or cardboard; attractive photos or pictures; yarn

Description of Activity

▪ Place the two dowels in the shape of a cross. Glue them together and secure the joint with wire, leaving enough wire to form a hook at the end. Hang the crossbar above the work area.

▪ Cut five three- or four-inch squares or rectangles out of construction paper or cardboard. Glue a picture to each side of the paper and attach them to the crossbars with yarn. The pictures can be attached with hot glue, or with regular glue if laid on a flat surface and allowed to dry.

Goals: Maintain and strengthen eye contact and ability to focus; provide visual stimulation; encourage conversation; maintain and improve ability to correctly label and verbalize objects

Picture Book

Stages: One through Three

Location: Inside or outdoors

Equipment: Photographs; pictures cut from magazines; construction paper of various colors—three-hole punched; paste or glue; three-ring binder

Description of Activity

- Choose a photograph for each page; then choose pictures from magazines that complement the picture. For example, to accompany a photograph taken at a park, select pictures of trees, birds, benches, fountains, and the like from magazines.
- Paste the selections to a piece of construction paper and insert it in the binder.
- Stimulate and encourage discussion by asking questions relating to the pictures.

Goals: Maintain and improve ability to correctly label and identify objects; strengthen eye contact and attention span; provide stimulus for conversation; utilize and strengthen memory recall; provide visual stimulation and distraction to people who are agitated

Adaptation: Place completed binders within easy reach so the loved one may pick up a book and look through it at his or her own pace. Ask the person to tell a short story about what is happening in a given picture and to identify colors, shapes, and objects.

Pinecone Wreath

Stages: One and Two

Location: Inside

Equipment: Newspaper; spool of thin florist's wire; pinecones in various sizes and in sufficient quantity to cover wreath form; wire cutters or pliers; liquid polymer, acrylic, or modge podge (a glue/shellac mixture); small shellac brushes; large brown plastic trash bag; scissors; twelve- or fourteen-inch Styrofoam wreath form; several U-shaped florist's pins; wired wooden florist's picks; about a dozen plastic seasonal decorations, small bows, or silk flowers; one large bow

Description of Activity

▪ Spread newspaper over the work area.

▪ Cut a nine-inch length of wire for each pinecone to be used.

▪ Wrap the end of a wire around the larger end of each pinecone as tightly as possible, twisting it several times to secure it to the cone. Leave several inches of wire, which will be used later to attach the cone to florist's picks.

▪ Paint each cone with a thin coat of polymer and set them on a rack or suspended by the wires from a clothesline. Allow to dry for approximately one to two hours or until no longer tacky.

▪ While the cones are drying, cut the trash bag into long strips, about three inches wide. Using as many strips as necessary, attach the end of a strip to the Styrofoam wreath form with a U-shaped florist's pin, and wrap the plastic around the form until it is completely covered. Secure the end of the strip to the form with a florist's pin.

■ Attach a florist's pick to each seasonal decoration and set them aside.

■ Wrap florist's wire around the top of the Styrofoam wreath and fashion a hoop for a hanger.

■ Attach a florist's pick to the large bow with florist's wire.

■ When the cones are dry, sort them into three sizes: large, medium, and small.

■ Attach a florist's pick to each cone by twisting the wire on the cone together with the wire on the pick.

■ Attach the largest cones to the outside of the wreath with florist's picks so that the outside is encircled. Just inside this circle, attach a row of medium cones, continuing until the circle is complete. Use the smallest cones to complete the inside of the wreath and to fill in any gaps

■ Attach decorations randomly around the wreath.

■ Attach the large bow to the bottom of the wreath.

Goals: Creation of an attractive, popular item for room decoration, gift, or bazaar

Adaptation: This can be a group activity—some people can collect pinecones, some can cut wire and paint the cones, and some can assemble the wreaths. It also makes a nice family project for all ages. Pinecones can be gathered during an outing or a nature walk around the yard, in a park, or wherever pinecones are available. Cones can be painted various colors with acrylic paints. The basic wreath-making process can be used to make wreaths using all silk flowers, bunches of dried flowers, and other variations. Smaller wreath forms can be used, and the wreaths can be adapted for all holidays.

Pom-Poms/Fuzz Balls

Stages: One through Three

Location: Inside or outdoors

Equipment: Cardboard; scissors; yarn

Description of Activity

▪ Cut out two doughnut-shaped pieces of cardboard about four inches in diameter with a hole in the middle about one inch in diameter.

▪ Cut several two- to three-foot lengths of yarn.

▪ Hold two cardboard doughnuts together so that the holes in the center line up. Starting at the center, hold one end of the yarn in place with your fingers or a bit of tape, then wrap the yarn around the doughnut, covering over the end of the yarn to secure it.

▪ Continue to wrap yarn around the doughnut until yarn is gone and cardboard is no longer visible. (Hint: If one piece of yarn is too short or you want to change colors, simply tie two pieces of yarn together and trim the ends.)

▪ With sharp scissors, cut the yarn along the outer edges of the two circles. The scissors will slide down between the two cardboard circles while you cut.

▪ Cut a piece of yarn about eight inches long. Wrap the yarn between the two layers of cardboard and draw it tight. Tie the yarn firmly into a knot.

▪ Being very careful not to cut the yarn, cut all the way through the cardboard to the center in several places. Gently pull the cardboard pieces loose from the pom-pom and fluff out yarn. The fuzzy ball now appears.

Goals: Exercise; social interaction; maintain and improve hand-eye coordination

Adaptation: This is another great activity to involve any children in the household. The ball can be used in games, as a decoration or an ornament, on a key chain, for luggage identification, and for many other purposes.

Potpourri

Stages: One and Two

Location: Inside or outdoors

Equipment: About a pound of rose petals and smaller amounts of other fragrant flower petals such as jasmine; tissue paper; three cups of salt; half-gallon container with lid; crushed dried herbs and spices such as rosemary, marjoram, cloves, mace, cinnamon, or coriander; pine needles; one ounce of violet sachet or essence of lavender; approximately one cup of rubbing alcohol

Description of Activity
▪ Spread the flower petals over the paper, sprinkle them with salt, and allow them to dry for several days.
▪ When the petals are dry, place them in the container. Add pinches of crushed herbs and spices and a sprinkling of broken pine needles. Add more salt and the essence of lavender.
▪ Sprinkle alcohol over the mixture and close the container tightly. Allow it to ferment for several weeks.

Goals: Fun; promote reminiscences of having made or used potpourri in the past

Adaptation: The potpourri can be placed around the house in containers, such as those that have been collaged in crafts, or sewed into small pillows to scent rooms, closets, and drawers. It also makes a good gift or bazaar item. The individual may choose to experiment with any variations of this recipe or may remember similar recipes from the past.

Rhythm Band Instruments

Stages: One through Three

Location: Inside or outdoors

Equipment: Hammer; nails; hole punch; rubber bands; string; glue; small blocks of wood; sandpaper; household and yard items; paint and brushes or other materials for adding decoration

Description of Activity

■ Drums. Almost any cylindrical cans or boxes can be used, such as empty paint cans and oatmeal boxes. Decorate as desired.

■ Drumsticks. Possibilities include small tree branches, wooden spoons, pencils, and chopsticks. Wad cloth or paper around the end of the stick to form a pad, and adhere it with a rubber band, string, or glue.

■ Tambourines. Use sturdy paper plates, paint can lids, or plastic lids. With a hole punch or hammer and nail, punch small holes around the edges. Flatten bottle caps with a hammer and punch a hole in the center with a hammer and nail. Next, tie a short string to one side of the bottle cap, and string through the holes in the paper plates, plastic lids, or paint can lids. Knot both ends securely. Decorate as desired.

- Rhythm sticks. Use bamboo rods, wooden dowels, large knitting needles—any sticks that can be hit together.
- Cymbals. If you have two old metal pot lids with knobs, you have a pair of cymbals.
- Sand blocks. Two small pieces of wood with sandpaper attached to one side are all you need. Rub the sandpaper sides together.
- Castanets. Fill coffee cans or baby food jars with small pebbles or dried beans. Secure lid. Shake.

Goals: Increase self-esteem; provide socialization with family members; maintain and improve fine motor coordination, sensory stimulation, and restorative skills; also a great way to include participation of children and bring out the "inner child" in all who join in

Ring Picture

Stages: One through Three

Location: Inside

Equipment: Wooden curtain rod ring; cardboard; pencil; scissors; Exacto knife; fabric scrap; glue; tiny dried flowers; ribbon

Description of Activity

■ Trace the inside of the wooden ring onto a piece of cardboard and cut the circle out using scissors or an Exacto knife.

■ Cut a piece of fabric from this cardboard pattern.

■ Take the ribbon and glue it to the cardboard circle. Then glue the fabric circle to the cardboard circle, sandwiching the ribbon.

■ Glue the cardboard side to the wooden ring.

■ Carefully glue the dried flowers to the fabric side of the ring, making an attractive design.

■ Make a knot in the free end of the ribbon to make a hanger.

■ Cut out a small picture and glue it to the cardboard side. The flower collage makes a delightful picture on the fabric side. You now have a two-sided hanging decoration.

Goals: Sense of satisfaction and pleasure from creating an attractive item; maintain and improve hand–eye coordination

Adaptation: This project can be adapted to make Christmas or other holiday decorations. Makes a nice gift.

Rock People

Stages: One and Two

Location: Inside or outdoors

Equipment: Round, smooth rocks of various sizes; glue; water-based paint; brushes; scraps of yarn and fabric

Description of Activity

- Clean the rocks.
- Glue an assortment of rocks together to make figures of various sizes and shapes. You can use a mixture of hot glue and a dab of regular glue for added strength. First apply the hot glue and attach the rocks; then apply regular glue to where the rock attaches to the hot glue.
- Paint and decorate the figures to look like people.

Goals: Stimulate the imagination with an amusing and creative activity; maintain and improve hand-eye coordination and restorative skills

Adaptation: Rocks can be made into various animal shapes as well as people. May be used as paperweights. Great project to do with kids.

Seed Collage

Stages: One and Two

Location: Inside, in-room

Equipment: Dried corn, peas, beans, and any other seeds of various sizes; glue or paste; construction paper

Description of Activity

- Spread glue over the paper with a brush. Sprinkle seeds onto the paper to form any picture or design desired. A picture may also be traced onto the paper and then filled in.

■ To prevent seeds from falling off, dry flat until fully fixed, approximately two to three hours.

■ Caution: Small beans may be ingested by persons in Stages Three and Four.

Goals: Individual achievement; self-expression; outlet for creativity; maintain and improve hand-eye coordination

Adaptation: Rice, grits, macaroni, or oatmeal with food coloring or tempera paint mixed with water may also be used. Spread the colored material on a flat surface to dry; several times during the day, stir through the particles to loosen them. When the material is completely dry, it can be stored in a plastic bag. To create the picture, spread glue on the construction paper. Dip or pour the material onto the paper. Shake off excess.

Spice Ball

Stages: One and Two

Location: Inside or outdoors

Equipment: Whole, unpeeled lemon or orange; sharp pencil; whole cloves; narrow ribbon

Description of Activity
■ Punch small holes all over the surface of the fruit with the pencil.
■ Insert a clove, stem first, into each hole.
■ Tie a piece of ribbon around the length of the fruit and another piece of ribbon around the width. Tie a long piece of

ribbon to a place where the two ribbons intersect so that the spice ball can be hung.

Goals: Satisfaction of creating a practical item that also can be used as a gift; maintain and improve hand-eye coordination

Adaptation: The project can be done in a group or by an individual. This old-fashioned pomander ball not only looks nice but also smells good and makes closets and drawers smell good too. Aroma enhances the appetite.

Sponge Painting

Stages: Three and Four

Location: Inside or outdoors

Equipment: Sponges; scissors; newspaper; heavy paper; tape; tempera or any water-based paints

Description of Activity

- Cut sponges into small pieces of various sizes and shapes.
- Cover work area with newspaper. Tape a sheet of heavy paper to the newspaper. Place small containers of paint within reach.
- Dip a piece of sponge lightly in the desired color of paint and then place the sponge on the paper to print a design. Use a different piece of sponge for each color of paint. Allow time for one color to dry before applying another color on top of it or nearby.

Goals: Use of creative talent; maintain and improve hand-eye coordination and cognitive skill of color identification; social activity

Adaptation: It might be advisable to sketch out the picture first so the person can follow the lines, but those who prefer to create their own pictures should be encouraged to do so. This project can be combined with collage technique for more elaborate pictures. Another great way to involve any children in the home.

Stenciling

Stages: One through Four

Location: Inside

Equipment: Stencil patterns; stock paper or poster paper; masking tape; acrylic paints and stencil brushes

Description of Activity

■ Select patterns that are big enough for easy stenciling. Either purchase patterns or make your own. If using purchased stencil patterns, carefully outline each pattern with a black permanent marker so that it is clear to someone with poor vision where the opening is. Patterns can easily be made from black construction paper. Make patterns that apply to a specific theme or holiday.

■ Tape the pattern down to the stock paper with masking tape.

■ Focus on one color of paint at a time. Use a spare sheet of paper to protect any areas that require a different color of paint.

Have the loved one stencil the first part of the pattern by dipping the stencil brush or any lightweight paint brush in the acrylic paint of choice and painting the area to be stenciled.

▪ When the first part is dry, remove the covering from the next area to be painted, cover up the area just painted, and allow the person to continue and to complete the picture.

Goals: Orient person to time; maintain and improve use of fine motor skills and cognitive skills, such as following one-step or two-step directions; enhance use of appropriate social skills; help restore and maintain color recognition

Adaptation: This activity is easily done with someone with a low level of functioning by giving the person hand-over-hand assistance, since materials are taped down. The hand-over-hand technique also provides an opportunity to bond and build trust. Stenciling can be done on any surface, such as wooden frames, cardboard, paper, and so on. Use this activity to make great picture frames either by stenciling directly on wooden frames or by cutting the center out of a nine-by-eleven-inch piece of cardboard and stenciling the border. The picture is merely taped to the back and you have fantastic picture frames with a personal touch.

Stuffed Animals

Stages: One and Two

Location: Inside

Equipment: Old nylon stockings, eight to ten pairs per animal; scissors; tracing paper and pencil; cotton fabric; sewing machine or needle and thread; marking pens or embroidery materials

Description of Activity

- Cut stockings into small pieces about a half inch long.
- Using tracing paper and a pencil, trace the accompanying cat pattern onto the wrong side of two pieces of fabric. Cut out the two forms.
- Sew the material wrong sides together around the edges as shown on the pattern, leaving the space between the *X*s open, and turn right side out.
- Stuff forms with cut-up stockings and whipstitch the open edges closed.
- Add features with marking pens or embroidery.

Goals: Render social service; enjoy companionship and a sense of achievement; maintain and improve hand-eye coordination, restorative skills, and ability to follow steps

Adaptation: Other simple animal patterns can be used as well. The animals can be adapted for holidays by using holiday colors. They make nice gifts for grandchildren, children's hospitals, and bazaars.

CAT PATTERN

Therapy Ball

Stages: One and Two (Three and Four with assistance)

Location: Inside or outdoors

Equipment: Old nylon stockings, one pair per ball; scissors; needle and thread

Description of Activity

■ Cut a ten-inch length from one leg of the stockings just above the ankle; cut the rest of the stockings into lengths of about two inches.

■ Tie a knot in one end of the ten-inch strip and turn the strip inside out.

■ Stuff the strip with the small stocking pieces to form a ball approximately the size of a tennis ball.

■ Make a knot in the other end of the ball and cut the ends off about an inch from the knot. With your thumb, push the knot down into the ball, and then sew the edges together to keep the ball tight and hide the knot.

Goals: Maintain and improve hand-eye coordination and restorative skills; therapy balls are helpful in maintaining hand strength, reducing stress, and providing a distraction activity to people in Stage Four during times of agitation

Adaptation: Therapy balls can be used in numerous games for fun and exercise. They can also be given to children's hospitals and day care centers.

Tissue Paper Collage

Stages: One and Two

Location: Better done inside

Equipment: Tissue paper in assorted colors; brushes, poster board or heavy art paper; polymer

Description of Activity

▪ Have loved one and family members tear colored tissue paper into pieces of assorted sizes and shapes.

▪ Paint a small area of poster board with polymer. Place a piece of torn paper on the wet polymer, and then paint over the paper with polymer. Continue the process of painting on the poster board with the polymer, putting torn paper on the board, and painting over it until the entire poster board is covered in this fashion.

Goals: Guaranteed success; self expression; therapeutic for anxious, nervous persons or family members

Adaptation: This project can range from simple to sophisticated depending on the ability of participants. The collage process can be applied to other bases as well to make decorative wastebaskets, vases, and other items. Paper can be torn or cut into any shape or design.

Tissue Paper Flowers

Stages: One through Three

Location: Inside or outdoors

Equipment: Colored tissue paper; scissors; florist's wire; pliers

Description of Activity

- For each flower, cut about five sheets of tissue paper to the size desired—five-inch pieces of different shapes and sizes work well.
- With the pliers, cut a length of florist's wire six to twelve inches for the stem.
- Put the sheets of tissue together, and accordion-fold them to form a narrow strip.
- Fold the strip in half to find the center. Cut a small "V" on each side of the center and wrap one end of the wire tightly around the notches several times.
- Gently separate each sheet of tissue to form the flower.

Goals: Diversion; self-expression; individual achievement; maintain and improve hand–eye coordination

Adaptation: Use more sheets of tissue to make flowers fuller. Flowers can be any size or color, stems can vary in length, and several can be put together for a bouquet or holiday decorations.

Wind Chimes

Stages: One through Four

Location: Inside

Equipment: Graduated plastic medicine containers with caps; ice pick or small hand drill; needle; four or five sections of fishing line, approximately twenty inches each; Mardi Gras beads; small cane stick

Description of Activity

- Punch a small hole through the tops of the medicine containers using an ice pick or small hand drill.
- Thread the needle with one section of fishing line. Draw the fishing line through the bottles alternately with a series of beads until desired length is reached. (Because of the dexterity required to thread the medicine bottles, stages Three and Four should hang beads only.)
- Knot the line and trim end, leaving approximately two inches at the other end for tying to the cane stick. Repeat with varied lengths.
- Tie several strings of bottles and beads to the cane stick. Hang on a porch or patio for everyone to enjoy.

Goals: Maintain and improve hand-eye coordination and ability to follow two-step and three-step directions; outlet for self-expression; enhance creative ability through meaningful activity

Community Outings

C ommunity outings with someone living with Alzheimer's or dementia can be a scary proposition for both the loved one and the caregiver. New situations can lead to confusion, fear, and agitation. The people under our care do not always act the way they did before the onset of symptoms. Therefore, when undertaking an outing, always go slowly and watch for signs of nervousness or agitation.

Following are some details with which loved ones may be able to assist depending on the stage they are currently in. Most tasks are appropriate for people in Stage One or Stage Two. However, those in Stages Three and Four may be able to pick destinations based on the pictures in brochures or advertisements in the phone book. The caregiver should also be at hand to supervise and assist as needed.

- Looking up phone numbers.
- Making phone calls—for example, to obtain information regarding hours of operation or admission fees, or to make reservations.
- Choosing food/refreshments and compiling shopping lists and checklists.
- Shopping for supplies.
- Preparing food/refreshments.
- Getting directions to the destination and locating it on a map.

Continuing with outings is an important aspect in maintaining social and cognitive skills, and when done according to the appropriate guidelines, it can be a pleasurable experience for everyone involved.

Location: The many possible destinations include local parks; shopping malls; cultural events such as plays, concerts, symphony performances, and university lectures; senior citizen lunches; zoos; fishing spots; craft and hobby stores; sporting events; nursing centers; ice cream and yogurt shops; libraries; bookstores; houses of worship; fairs; school events; bowling alleys; meetings of social groups; movies; museums; art exhibits; parades; and political rallies as well as rides by car, bus, boat, or other means.

Equipment: Varies—make a checklist of items you'll want

Description of Activity
- Begin preparations several days in advance.
- Involve the loved one in decisions as to location, menu, what to do, and other details.
- Stress the importance of working together and doing what needs to be done before, during, and after the outing.

■ Check out the chosen site before you go so you will know the area, what's available, and conditions of using the facilities.

■ Make any necessary transportation arrangements.

■ If you have doubts about being able to handle the person under your care, start slowly with short, simple outings prior to attempting a larger outing to test your ability to handle the responsibilities that will be involved.

■ Have emergency procedures worked out for unexpected events such as illness or injury.

■ Make sure the person carries a card in a pocket or wallet with his or her name, address, and phone number on it. Make sure you have with you a recent photo of the person so that you are prepared if he or she should wander off.

■ Depending on the situation, it's often a good idea to have a wheelchair on hand (e.g., in the trunk of your car) for emergencies.

■ Take a first aid kit and any medications the loved one may need.

■ Have plenty of snack foods to serve as a distraction if the person becomes anxious.

■ Take extra clothing, depending on the scope of the outing.

■ Make sure the loved one has pocket money if it will be necessary to make purchases. It can be embarrassing for the person to have to ask for money. Even though you may often need to provide direction for making purchases, it increases the person's self-esteem to purchase items independently.

■ Take photographs en route to and from the destination and during the visit. These pictures make great additions to any photo album and can enhance retention of the memories. Also make a point to pick up and retain any handouts, printed programs, and other souvenirs from the trip.

▪ If others are involved in the outing, thank them all for their help and participation. Expressing your feelings of joy for time spent outside the home will greatly increase the loved one's self-esteem and confidence in future outings.

Goals: Provide the experience of "normal" community activities; motivate positive thinking about the person's relationship to the environment and the community; socialize with the caregiver as well as with people in the community; stimulate mental processes of interest, enthusiasm, memory, hope, learning, and enjoyment; enhance feelings of self-worth

Adaptation: Often, people with Alzheimer's or dementia exhibit behavior problems due to fear or nervousness. If you find yourself in the position of having to explain to concerned onlookers that the person has Alzheimer's or dementia, you are likely to embarrass the person. To avoid this situation, the accompanying card may be cut out and laminated and carried with you so that you can quietly show it to people who express concern about the loved one's behavior without causing embarrassment to anyone.

Please do not be alarmed. The person I am with has Alzheimer's and is only acting this way because he/she is nervous. He/She is not a threat to you or himself/herself. Thank you for your patience and understanding.

Exercise

What you don't use, you lose. This is true of both our physical and mental capacities. Many people with Alzheimer's or dementia have difficulty moving about simply because they have little opportunity for physical activity. An exercise program can tone muscles, improve circulation, limber up the body, and relieve tension.

General Suggestions
- Before beginning any exercises, make sure everyone is wearing appropriate clothing that will allow for free movement, and remove any jewelry or glasses. Also be sure to have plenty of water on hand.
- Plan the exercise program in conjunction with the person's physician. People with Alzheimer's should participate only with their physician's approval.

- The more people involved, the better. This is a great way for everyone in the house, including children, to become more active.
- A good time to do exercises is before meals—or wait at least an hour after a meal.
- Start with a few simple exercises, and increase the number and type as the person can tolerate them.
- Do each exercise slowly. This will increase its benefit and give the loved one an opportunity to understand the purpose of the exercise.
- Encourage the loved one to do a few simple arm and leg exercises independently each morning and night.
- Throwing beach balls or beanbags around is a fun way to get the body moving.
- End each session with a glass of ice water and some good conversation.

Keep in mind that the person's ability to engage in physical activities may be limited. Some people need to participate in a modified manner or perhaps only as a spectator. All exercises can be done sitting or standing because you are exercising the joints of the wrists, elbows, forearms, shoulders, and hips. Straightback chairs should be used, preferably without armrests. If the loved one is in a wheelchair, make sure the wheels are locked, and then, if possible, place the person's feet on the floor and loosen the wheelchair seat belt. There is some debate on whether to start with the upper body or lower body; again, check with the loved one's physician for the proper sequence of exercises. Have comfortable chairs nearby for frequent rest periods, and always have plenty of water and towels available.

Procedure

- Bring everyone together in a group where space permits, such as in a living room or on a patio. Outdoors would be preferable or anyplace that will provide fresh air and good ventilation. Remember, however, that exercising in hot weather can cause dehydration and episodes of hypotension (low blood pressure).
- Make sure there is plenty of room to perform exercises and remove any objects that could be hazardous and cause injury or get broken. Again make sure the person has water nearby for adequate hydration.
- Scheduling sessions before lunch can work well, since people often are already together, or evenings may be preferable to promote sleep.
- Have exercises well in mind. Try not to read from a paper.
- One person should lead and give all instructions. Helpers, such as children in the household, should follow the leader.
- Leaders should ensure that they have the participants' attention before carrying out an exercise.
- Do each exercise about five times to start, increasing the number of repetitions as familiarity and tolerance increase. Anyone who becomes tired during a routine can stop and rest.
- Exercise periods should last from fifteen to twenty-five minutes, depending on the persons involved.
- Many people enjoy playing catch or kicking a ball as part of the exercise routine. This should take additional time—ten to twenty minutes—again depending on the persons involved.

- Be enthusiastic! Enjoy the exercises yourself. Present the exercises in an adult manner.
- It is a good idea to take frequent breaks during any exercise program. During these rest periods, initiate reality-oriented discussions regarding the weather, the day's news, birthdays, or similar topics.

Are We Ready? Warm-Ups

It is essential to perform warm-up exercises to prevent injuries to the muscles and tendons. Arthritis and general stiffness can cause injuries to muscles that are not properly warmed up prior to the exercise routine. In fact, warming up is so important that it should be done daily in the morning and at night. It helps to reduce stiffness and promotes a more restful sleep pattern.

Breathing
- Raise arms forward and up while breathing in. Lower arms sideways and down while breathing out.
- With hands clasped on top of the head, breathe in, lifting the chest. Breathe out while relaxing.
- With arms straight down at the sides, breathe in while lifting and rolling the arms out with the inside of the arm facing up. Breathe out as arms relax and return to starting position.
- With hands clasped behind the neck and elbows facing front, breathe in while moving elbows to the sides. Breathe out as the elbows move back to the starting position.

Deep Breathing

- Stand or sit tall. Breathe in deeply through the nostrils, trying to fill the belly with air. Let air out slowly through the mouth.

Breathing Stretches

- Stand or sit tall. Stretch arms toward the ceiling, rising on tiptoes. Bend at the waist and let the air out while stretching down.

Swimming Strokes

- While sitting or standing, move arms in a swimming motion. Start with each arm straight out in front. Then bring down to the side, around the back with elbow bent, and return to the starting position. Alternate arms. "Swim" for thirty seconds to a minute.

Arm Circles

- Sitting or standing with arms extended at the sides, make large circles with the arms without bending the elbows. Circle forward and backward, varying the size of the circles.

Exercises

Now that we're all warmed up, it's time for the exercise program. Here are just a few suggestions to exercise each part of the body. Pick one or two from each section to customize the program. Again, always check with your loved one's physician for appropriate exercises and their sequence.

Exercises for Head and Neck

Chest Touches

■ Touch the chin to the chest, and then roll the head backward, with chin raised to the ceiling. If this causes dizziness for participants, tell them to focus on a point straight in front of them during the movement. They should stop and look at this point briefly each time they face forward.

Ear Touches

■ Roll the head from side to side in a straight line, attempting to touch the ear to the shoulder.

Chin Stretches

■ With head erect, jut the chin out and move jaws up and down.

Exercises for Face and Neck

■ Move the head in a circle.
■ Lift the crown of the head toward the ceiling, keeping the chin parallel with the floor. Do not bend the head backward.
■ Stretch the face into varying contortions. For example, raise eyebrows as high as possible; smile as widely as possible; fill the cheeks with air and hold them puffed out; pucker for a few seconds.
■ Chew gum.

- When outdoors or near an open window, blow bubbles—the bubble water and wand can be purchased at party stores or grocery stores.

Exercises for Trunk

- With hands on hips, twist first one way and then the other.
- Start with hands at the sides. Now reach down with both hands and reach for the knees, first one side and then the other.
- A participant in a wheelchair can do "Wheelchair Push-Ups": with hands on the arms of the chair and feet on the floor, lift the buttocks off the chair momentarily. (Be sure to first lock the wheelchair brakes!)

Exercises for Midsection

Toe Touches
- While sitting or standing, stretch the arms up, and then bend over and try to touch the toes. Bending knees is permissible.

Bends
- With hands on the waist, bend forward and then to each side and then backward. Put lots of stretch into this.

Bounces
- Put one hand on the waist, and let the other arm hang straight from the side. Gently bend with a bouncing

motion, trying to touch the floor with your fingers. Repeat this up-and-down motion several times to the same side, then alternate sides.

Pectoral Stretches

- Place the hands behind the neck, move the elbows back, and perform a breaststroke motion.

Exercises for Arms, Shoulders, and Upper Back

Arm Exercises

- Clench fists.
- Bounce a basketball. First dribble in place, then bounce to another person.
- Throw a basketball from the chest.
- Bounce a ball from overhead: hold the ball overhead and release it.
- With arms forward and elbows straight, bend sideways at the waist, first to the right and then to the left.
- Using a tennis racket or Ping-Pong paddle, bat a small Nerf ball.
- Place hands on the shoulders, stretch them in the air, place them back on the shoulders, and then lower them.
- With arms at the sides and elbows straight, roll arms out with palms up; rotate palms up and down.
- Turn the palms up and down.

Shoulder Shrugs

- While sitting or standing, with arms hanging at sides, raise both shoulders simultaneously as if trying to touch the shoulders to the ears.

Hand Swings

- While standing or sitting at the forward edge of a chair, stretch the hands straight out in front of the body, and then swing the arms down and as far back as possible. Try to touch hands together behind the body.

Alternate Swings

- While standing or sitting at the forward edge of a chair, put one arm in front of the body and one arm in back. Swing forward and backward, keeping both arms going in opposite directions.

Touches

- While standing or sitting, place hands on the shoulders, raise arms in the air, touch the shoulders again, stretch arms out to the sides, touch the shoulders again, stretch arms to the front, and touch the shoulders again.

Wood Chopping

- Move one arm vigorously in a chopping motion, with the fist clenched. Do this for one minute and then switch hands.

Rooster Flaps

- While sitting or standing, lift the arms straight out to the sides, bend at the elbows, and place hands in armpits. Stretch bent arms front to back, like a rooster flapping its wings.

Exercises for the Hands

Fist Clenches

- Clench hands tightly in a fist and then release fingers explosively, stretching them out as far as you can.

Wrist Shakes

- Pull the hands close to the chest and shake them vigorously. The action should come from the wrists.

Finger Bounces

- Hold your hands with fingertips together and palms facing each other. Pull hands apart approximately three inches, then quickly touch the tips of the fingers again. Do this in a bouncing, rhythmic motion for at least one minute.

Ball Squeezes

- Alternating hands, squeeze a small rubber ball or tennis ball firmly, and then release.

Exercises for Ankles and Feet

Ankle Circles

- Cross the right leg over the left leg. With the right ankle, make circles going to the right and then circles going to the left. Switch legs and make circles in both directions with the left foot. This exercise is great when done to music.

Ankle Stretches

■ While sitting in a chair, hold both legs together off the floor, straight out in front of the body. Point toes toward floor and then flex them back toward the knees.

Exercises for Legs

Leg Exercises—Sitting

■ Alternating feet, tap toes on the floor. This is another exercise that is exellent for doing to music.
■ Rock up on the toes, and then rock back on the heels.
■ Alternating legs, kick with the knee straight.
■ Marching in place, lift alternate feet off the ground.

Knee Raises

■ Sitting or standing, bend the right leg and touch the knee to the chest, and then do the same with the left leg.

Leg Raises

■ While sitting, raise the right leg straight in front of the body and then lower it, keeping leg straight. Do this several times, and then repeat with the left leg.

Marching

■ March in place, raising knees high. Hold onto back of a chair if necessary for balance.

Swinging Legs

- Holding onto the back of a chair with the left hand, swing the right leg forward and then back. Move to the other side of the chair, hold on with the right hand, and swing the left leg forward and backward.

Leg Circles

- Holding onto the back of a chair with the left hand, raise the right leg toward the front and keep it straight while moving it in circles. Switch sides, and do the same with the left leg.

After Exercises

Toss a beanbag around and enjoy good conversation!

Exercise Program

Trying to customize an exercise program can be hard when you are just beginning. This sample program is appropriate for all stages and can be your model. Most exercises can be done with a group or individually.

Stages: One through Four

Location: Use a large room. Many aging people have limited space in their daily routine. Exposing them to a large room expands the spirit, allowing them the opportunity to really "let go"; plus some of the following exercises demand space.

Equipment: Music; bicycle inner tubes

Description of Activity

■ The sequence is warm-ups/stretching—briefly moving each body part (see "Are We Ready? Warm-Ups" earlier in this chapter); endurance exercises—which are more active; and then cooldown—uplifting, something slow and fun.

■ Keep the time interesting! Treat each exercise as a single entity. Mix and match according to the focus of the individual. Linger on the successful exercises, and cut short the faltering ones. Use ordinary equipment (such as inner tubes and brooms) to add accent.

■ Explain the benefit of each exercise. Don't do meaningless, repetitive exercises. Do interesting, purposeful exercises.

■ Use music. Choose music appropriate to the individual exercise. Music that helps keep the beat or that sets the mood is good.

■ Some exercises don't require music, so turn it off.

Warm-Ups

■ Stand side by side with the one you are caring for and hold hands (this helps with balance). If you have more than two people, stand in a circle and hold hands.

■ All walk right; all walk left. This improves reactions and ability to follow directions while providing gentle arm stretching as well as warming up slowly. Use your imagination to continue warm-ups in a nonthreatening manner.

Random Walking

■ Each person randomly walks around the room. Start slowly, then pick up the pace. After a while, you and your loved one will be avoiding collisions, which improves coordination.

■ Use your imagination and add details such as swinging arm movements or clapping to the music.

Inner Tubes

■ You may be able to get old inner tubes for free from a bike shop. Place the tubes on the floor at random and do "random walking." Ask the person not to step inside the tubes—perhaps pretend they are puddles to avoid. This activity improves coordination and reactions by forcing participants to vary their step length.

Line Patterns

■ Stand side by side on one side of the room. In unison, walk across the room in a pattern step—for example: three steps forward, one step back, three steps forward, one step back.

Back Rub

■ Older people tend to lose the routine physical contact they had in their younger relationships. This exercise is a fun way to renew some normal physical contact. Stand shoulder to shoulder with the one under your care. First turn to the right and rub the back of that person, then turn to the left and repeat. Enjoy!

Goals: Maintain activity; maintain and improve coordination, balance, ability to follow two-step to three-step directions, and—most of all—a healthy body

Gross Motor Exercise

Stages: One through Four

Location: This is a great exercise program to hold outdoors, but it can be performed anywhere that chairs can comfortably fit side by side.

Equipment: Rubber ball or Nerf ball; canes or similar items that can be used to bat a ball; simple game equipment to toss, such as beanbags and plastic hoops

Terminology: Following is a list of terminology used in the range-of-motion exercises (see also figure on next page)

- Adduction—movement of a limb or digits toward the medial or axial plane of the body
- Abduction—a lateral movement of a limb away from the medial plane of the body
- Extension—a movement that brings the members of a limb toward a straight condition
- Dorsiflexion—movement of a part at a joint so as to bend the part toward the posterior aspect (back) of the body
- Flexion—the act of bending or being bent inward
- Hyperextension—a movement that brings the members of a limb beyond a straight condition
- Plantar flexion—extension of the foot so that the forepart is depressed in respect to the position of the ankle
- Pronation—turning the palm or foot to face down or backward
- Supination—turning the palm or foot upward

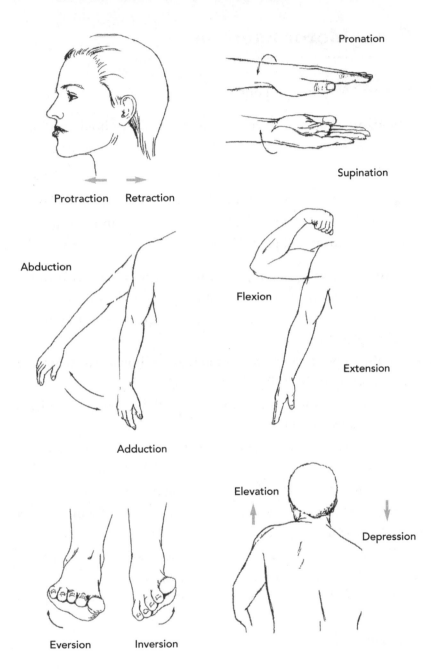

Pronation

Supination

Protraction   Retraction

Abduction

Flexion

Extension

Adduction

Elevation

Depression

Eversion   Inversion

RANGE-OF-MOTION EXERCISES

Fingers

- Flexion—curl fingers inward, making a fist
- Extension—stiffen hand and fingers straight up
- Hyperflexion—bend fingers backward and outward
- Adduction—pull fingers tight together
- Abduction—spread fingers out

Wrist

- Flexion—bend wrist downward
- Extension—bend wrist backward
- Hyperextension—bend wrist backward as far as you can go without causing pain
- Ulnar deviation—bend wrist outward to the side
- Radial deviation—bend wrist inward toward the middle

Forearm

- Flexion—bend elbows inward toward the body
- Extension—extend elbow straight out with palms of hands facing upward
- Pronation—extend arms out to the side and rotate arms inward
- Supination—extend arms out to the side and rotate arms upward, palms facing up

Shoulder

- Flexion—roll shoulder inward
- Extension—roll shoulder backward
- Hyperextension—roll shoulder backward as far as possible without causing pain
- Abduction—keep arm straight, lift arm straight out to side at shoulder level
- Adduction—pull both arms tight next to the body
- Elevation—shrug shoulder upward

- Depression—push shoulder downward
- Horizontal abduction—holding arm straight out at shoulder level, move arm backward
- Horizontal adduction—holding arm straight out at shoulder level, cross arm in front

Hip
- Flexion—bend forward
- Extension—bend backward. (If in a chair, sit near edge to allow some backward movement, make sure that feet are firmly touching the floor.)

Ankle
- Plantar flexion—stretch feet upward, pointing toes toward the ceiling
- Dorsal flexion—stretch feet downward, pointing toes down

Description of Activity
- The setting should be informal, with everyone seated. Arrange chairs side by side, in a circle, or in a horseshoe.
- Start by orienting to the day of the week, date, and weather.
- Describe what type of activities a person might do this time of year.
- Begin with various range-of-motion exercises (as described above) to move joints: fingers—flexion and extension, adduction and abduction; wrist—flexion and extension, hyperextension, ulnar and radial deviation; elbow—flexion and extension; forearm—pronation and supination; shoulder—flexion and extension, hyperextension, abduction and adduction, elevation and depression, horizontal abduction and adduction; hip—flexion and extension; ankle—dorsal flexion and plantar flexion.
- Play catch, with the leader tossing a ball to each person, who tries to catch it and then toss it back to the leader.

■ Play simple circle games, such as using the end of a cane to hit a rubber ball across the floor to each other or tossing plastic hoops to each other.

■ Vary exercises from week to week.

Goals: Maintain and improve active range of motion, number and simple math concepts, up/down and left/right discrimination, imitation of body movements, and direction-following skills; improve body image and body parts identification; provide opportunity for appropriate group interaction; reinforce reality orientation, especially person-to-person

Adaptation: Be sure to check with a family physician to determine the person's physical limitations, as carelessness can cause injury. The program should last thirty to forty-five minutes. Provide ample rest periods. The program can be split into several short periods each day. Late afternoons tend to be a successful time. This is a good program to start with; add to it as you and the loved one gain strength and confidence.

Balloon Beach Ball Games

Stages: One through Four

Location: Inside or outdoors—with adequate space for swinging the bat and kicking the ball

Equipment: Beach ball; newspaper bat—roll several sections of newspaper together for strength, and tape the seam; balloon or punching balloon

Description of Activity

Catch and Volley

▪ The leader and participant toss or volley the beach ball back and forth a few times. If necessary, explain how to volley. If you're doing this in a group, go around the circle, calling each person by name before his or her turn—to make sure you have the person's attention!

▪ Depending on the ability level of the participants, you can ask or tell the person to toss or volley the ball to one of the other members of the group. You can also kick the ball back and forth.

Beach Ball Baseball

▪ The leader and participant(s) can alternate roles as pitcher, hitter, and catcher/fielder. The hitter uses as much force as possible to hit the ball with the newspaper bat.

Kick Ball

▪ Place the beach ball or balloon on the floor and encourage everyone involved to kick the ball to each other.

Goals: Exercise arms and legs; encourage social interaction; elicit enthusiasm and reflex actions; maintain and improve hand–eye coordination

In-Chair Dancing

This is a great addition to any program and is especially suited to people with disabilities or low levels of endurance.

Stages: One through Three (Stage Four with assistance)

Location: Inside

Equipment: Props such as scarves, flags, flowers, instruments, canes, or dowel rods (optional); music—fast and slow (your imagination is the limit!)

Description of Activity

- All participants do this while seated. For groups, arrange participants in a semicircle with yourself in the middle; if this is a one-on-one activity, sit opposite each other.
- If you're using props, allow participants to choose.
- Turn on the music, and lead in moving to the beat. It is not necessary for everyone to be doing the same thing at the same time.
- Observe for any signs of fatigue.
- Alternate between slow music and fast. Start out slowly, and gradually speed things up. Before stopping, slow things down again to allow for a cooldown period.
- Don't set yourself up for frustration by expecting anyone with Alzheimer's to follow a choreographed dance routine. Know what movements or exercises are possible, and simply have fun with them. You must supply the energy and enthusiasm.
- Try theme dances such as square dancing, country and western line dancing, or hula dances with Hawaiian music. Let everyone be creative!
- Some music may be enjoyable to one person but upsetting to another. Be alert to reactions and modify your music selection accordingly.

Goals: Promote physical movement and exercise; maintain and improve hand-eye coordination and gross motor coordination;

positive and constructive release of nervous anxiety; social enjoyment and positive interaction between caregiver and loved one

Basketball

Stages: One through Three

Location: Inside or outdoors

Equipment: Wastebasket or fruit basket; beanbags

Description of Activity

▪ Place basket in center of play area, with participants positioned around a circle a set distance from the basket. The game can be played by either teams or individuals competing against each other.

▪ Each person takes a turn tossing a beanbag twice and trying to get it into the basket. The game continues until either a set score has been obtained or the play has progressed a set number of times around the circle.

Goals: Mild exercise; enjoyment of competition; maintain and improve hand–eye coordination and socialization skills

Beanbag Toss

Stages: One through Three

Location: Inside or outdoors

Equipment: Three beanbags; box for target board

Description of Activity

▪ To make the target board, cut three holes in the bottom of a medium-size box. Holes should be large enough for beanbags to fit through. Cut the box so that it will be on a diagonal when set on the floor. The game follows the rules of traditional beanbags.

▪ Arrange players in a circle around the target board or directly in front with only one or two players.

▪ Each player throws three beanbags.

▪ Scores are totaled up after each player's turn.

▪ The game may be played with individuals competing against each other or in teams.

▪ The game ends when a set score is reached or when everyone has had a set number of turns.

Goals: Mild exercise; enjoyment of competition; maintain and improve hand-eye coordination and socialization skills

Food-Oriented
Activities

All that's needed for these activities is a small kitchen area where the loved one and caregiver can prepare simple meals, along with a few basic ingredients and implements. With a little ingenuity, you can devise methods of allowing the person for whom you're caring to enjoy simple activities related to food preparation. And, of course, everyone remembers the smells of Mama's kitchen—the aromas alone can be a source of pleasure. Knowing just how much a person can do is the tricky part. This chapter gives you some ideas and recipes that are practically foolproof, no matter what the stage of the cook.

Ideas

- Before you begin, remember to have everyone who participates carefully wash their hands before handling any food items.

- This is a perfect time for one-to-one chats. Any type of cooking activity will bring back memories from childhood and early adulthood. Most people at some point have sat around a table, either preparing or eating food, and it is a good, relaxing time to share these memories.

- When selecting a recipe, check for any food allergies, such as milk, lemon, chocolate, vanilla, nut, or other food allergies.

- At a table or counter, assemble the ingredients and equipment for a simple recipe such as cookies, a cake, or a personal favorite. The loved one can mix the ingredients, and then the caregiver can do any cooking or baking.

- Purchase fresh peas, beans, or corn in season for the loved one to shell or shuck either inside or on the patio or lawn.

- People in Stages One and Two who are able and interested can peel potatoes, apples, and similar foods, but always monitor the activity, since sharp tools can cause injury.

- Ask the loved one to write down any favorite recipes, or use a tape recorder and then transcribe the instructions. The loved one could also dictate the recipe to the caregiver.

- Write or type a favorite recipe on a decorated or colored index card for the loved one to give to relatives or other visitors.
- Compile a simple family cookbook.

Edible Art

Stages: One through Three (Stage Four with assistance)

Location: Kitchen

Equipment: Waxed paper; tray; yogurt, pudding, or jam; granola or chocolate chips; music

Description of Activity

- Place a sheet of waxed paper on a tray and situate the tray in front of the loved one. If this is a group activity, have a tray for each participant. Allow the person to choose an "edible paint"—yogurt, pudding, or jam.
- Place a serving portion of the chosen "edible paint" on the waxed paper and encourage the loved one to finger paint with it. Granola or chocolate chips can be used to complete the picture. Assist when necessary.
- Use music to help stimulate movement in painting.
- The real fun begins when the artwork is done to their liking; then it is time to dig in and eat the masterpiece.

Goals: Stimulate senses of touch, taste, and smell; encourage socialization and awareness of others if this is a group activity; provide extra nourishment in the form of a snack

Adaptive Cooking: Pudding

Stages: One through Three (Stage Four with hand–over–hand assistance)

Location: Kitchen

Equipment: Instant pudding mix; milk; liquid measure; one-pound coffee can with plastic lid or other closed container; cups or bowls; spoons and napkins

Description of Activity

- Assemble all the items on a table or other area easily seen by the loved one.
- Introduce the activity by explaining what is going to be prepared. Ask for the loved one's memories of making pudding in the past—perhaps over a hot stove, stirring and stirring! Ask for help when you measure out the milk and put it into the container, and then add the pudding mix according to the instructions on the box.
- Seal the container securely.
- Ask the loved one and any other participants to give the container a few shakes to combine the powdered mix with the milk.
- Assist when necessary. (Make sure the lid is on securely!)
- After the pudding is thoroughly mixed, let the loved one help pour it into individual bowls or cups.
- Enlist the loved one's help in serving the refreshment and distributing spoons and napkins.

Goals: Stimulate senses of touch, taste, and smell; encourage socialization and awareness of others if this is a group activity; provide extra nourishment in the form of a snack; stimulate memories of cooking, meal preparation, and serving, which can lead to discussion

Variations: The same procedure can be followed using powdered drinks. An advantage to this activity is that it requires no cooking and therefore poses little safety risk to the loved one. Depending on ability level, some people may just be passive participants (watching) while others will be more actively involved.

Cake Decorating

Stages: One and Two

Location: Kitchen

Equipment: Any type of cake mix or homemade recipe that can be baked in a jelly roll pan or made into cupcakes (cupcakes may promote increased interaction and expressions of creativity); tubes of colored icing with decorating tips; spatulas

Description of Activity

- Invite the loved one to join you around the cake or cupcakes to apply the frosting.
- Suggest making a creative design in the center. Cake icing can be smoothed on with a spatula, or experiment with dipping the tip of the spatula in different colored icing and dabbing it on. Plastic bristle brushes also work well for persons of decreased dexterity.
- Encourage the loved one to help with cutting the cake if appropriate and arranging servings.

Goals: Sensory and creative stimulation; encourage socialization; maintain and improve hand-eye coordination

Adaptation: This is another good way to involve children in the household as well as a special way to celebrate a birthday.

Cracker Decorating

Stages: One through Three

Location: Kitchen

Equipment: Crackers; several varieties of aerosol cheese spread

Description of Activity

■ Place the crackers and cheese spread containers on a decorative, nonbreakable plate.

■ Encourage the loved one to press the nozzle on the cheese can to form designs on the crackers.

■ Prompt the person to discuss favorite flavors or reminisce about a time or place when he or she shared a similar snack with someone.

■ The crackers should be eaten as soon as they are decorated. (It is also pleasant to serve them with some juice.)

Goals: Sensory and creative stimulation; encourage socialization, maintain and improve hand-eye coordination; combine an activity with a snack to stimulate the appetite, since people with Alzheimer's often have a poor appetite

Vegetable Prints

Stages: One through Three (Stage Four with hand–over–hand assistance)

Location: Kitchen or outdoors

Equipment: Heavy wrapping paper or newspaper; three colors of tempera paints (nontoxic, washable); three pie tins; carrots and potatoes cut into interesting shapes, such as triangles, diamonds, doughnuts, or flowers; white construction paper; paper towels

Description of Activity
■ Cover the work area with heavy wrapping paper or newspaper.
■ Put a small amount of paint in each pie tin —one color per tin. Place the vegetable shapes near the paint tins on the work table.
■ Give the loved one a sheet of construction paper.
■ Demonstrate how the vegetable is dipped into the paint and then pressed onto the paper.
■ Press the used piece onto paper toweling to soak up the paint before dipping it into a different color.

Goals: Sensory stimulation; maintain and improve hand–eye coordination and restorative skills such as remembering colors

Ice Cream Party: Make Your Own Sundae

Stages: One through Three

Location: Kitchen or outdoors

Equipment: Ice cream mixture (sample recipe follows); ice cream freezers—hand-cranked and electric; serving/mixing spoons; ice cream scoops; bowls and spoons; pushcart for distributing toppings (optional); music (optional)

Description of Activity

- Make sure a suitable table and a sufficient number of chairs are available in the location. Enlist others as needed to help with preparations and serving.

- Prepare the ice cream mixture (diabetic or regular) ahead of time, adjusting quantities to accommodate expected number of guests.

- Set up hand-cranked and electric freezers, and make the ice cream according to instructions on the freezers. Involve the loved one in the process where possible—putting in the ice, adding salt, cranking, and so forth.

- When the ice cream is ready, scoop it into bowls and distribute it to guests. If necessary, some bowls of ice cream can be prescooped and placed in the kitchen freezer a few minutes before the party.

- As soon as bowls are distributed, have someone circulate with toppings, perhaps using a pushcart.

- About an hour should be allowed for the party, which could be centered around a theme or season, such as ragtime music or the Fourth of July. Entertainment, music, and decorations corresponding to the theme can also be included.

Goals: Provide a beneficial social function; stimulate positive reminiscing; provide an opportunity to make choices; maintain and improve socialization skills and hand-eye coordination; provide a calming atmosphere for those who may get agitated easily

Ice Cream for Low-Calorie and Diabetic Diets

1 envelope unflavored gelatin

2 tablespoons cold water

⅔ cup dry skim milk solids (such as Pet or Carnation)

2 cups water

½ cup sugar

¼ teaspoon salt

2 cups evaporated skim milk (canned)

2 teaspoons vanilla

Soften the gelatin in the cold water.

Combine the milk solids and 2 cups water in a small pot, and scald the mixture. Add the softened gelatin, sugar, and salt. Stir until gelatin and sugar are dissolved. Cool. Add evaporated skimmed milk and vanilla.

Freeze according to directions for ice cream freezer.

Makes about 1 quart, or 8 half-cup servings.

Nutritional Information: One-half cup serving contains 21.5 grams carbohydrates; 6 grams protein; 108 calories; and 0 grams fat.

Fresh fruits such as peaches, strawberries, and pineapple may be added for flavor. Nutritional information must be adjusted accordingly.

Games

Recreational activities are a normal part of everyone's life and are necessary for a sense of well-being. Recreation promotes health through physical exercise, social contact, and increased self-confidence. Fun and games relieve boredom, provide something to anticipate, and just generally enrich the quality of life available to the loved one at home, who often feels left out because of Alzheimer's.

In addition to providing a competitive outlet for aggression and frustration, games set up a social situation in which persons with Alzheimer's can express themselves in a relaxed and open manner. Playing games also promotes listening skills and active group participation and improves hand-eye coordination.

Recreational activities can promote increased self-esteem and allow for increased participation in the community, such as Senior Olympics and chess tournaments. Skill acquisition, however, is always secondary to the social, emotional, and physical benefits derived from recreational activities.

Ideas

- Traditional board games such as checkers, chess, and Monopoly
- Card games—caregivers are encouraged to purchase a card game book to learn a variety of games to be played with the loved one
- Velcro darts
- Horseshoes or silver dollar throw
- Exercise class for people who are ambulatory, use wheelchairs, or are bed-bound
- Relaxation exercises
- Parties—large and small
- Competitive tournaments, contests, leagues for board games and active games such as darts and horseshoes
- Silly hat contests
- Guessing games—challenge the person living with Alzheimer's to estimate how many pennies or beans are in a jar; the person drops guesses into a box every day until the correct number is guessed and then is rewarded with a special outing or treat
- A field day with many outdoor activities: wheelchair races, Frisbee throws, tetherball, basketball toss; involve the whole family in creating special events
- Wheelchair square dancing and traditional square dancing
- Lawn games such as croquet and badminton

- Kites
- Senior Olympics—encourage practice prior to the competition, and conduct elimination contests for events
- Dances with bands, accordion players, and so forth
- Field trips in the community—bowling alleys, events for senior citizens, festivals, spectator sports
- Swimming—arrange to use a community or college pool at specific times if no home pool is available
- Modified golf, driving range, putting green

Additional games, with specific information for each, are included in this section.

Balloon Volleyball

Stages: One through Three

Location: Inside or outdoors—this is a great way to involve even the smallest children in the house

Equipment: Net or cord; large, brightly colored balloons

Description of Activity
- Suspend the net or cord between two poles or walls at a height of four to four and a half feet from the ground.
- Blow up the balloons.
- Divide the players into two teams.
- Play starts when the server taps a balloon into the air, trying to send it to the opposite side of the net or cord. If the attempt is not successful, two more taps are allowed by other players. If

the team fails to get the balloon over the net or cord within three taps, or if the balloon touches the floor, the balloon is passed to the other team for play.

■ Only the serving team is eligible to score. If the receiving team fails to return the balloon, the serving team scores.

Goals: Exercise; recreation; maintain and improve hand-eye coordination

Adaptation: Players may rotate positions. A regular volleyball may be used instead of balloons if all players have suitable strength.

Beanbag Basketball

Stages: One through Three

Location: Inside or outdoors—a perfect activity for younger children to join in

Equipment: Cardboard; wire coat hanger; large-holed nylon mesh such as a laundry bag; beanbag

Description of Activity

■ To make the basketball hoop, cut a piece of cardboard in the shape of a backboard. Straighten out the coat hanger and weave through the top of the nylon mesh. Attach the hanger to the cardboard—be sure the opening is large enough for the beanbag to easily slip through it.

▪ Divide the players into two teams. Establish a throw line. The players on the two teams alternate tossing the beanbag. Each player has three tries to throw the beanbag through the hoop.

▪ The scoring is as follows: A goal on the first try earns 3 points; a goal on the second try earns 2 points; and a goal on the third try earns 1 point.

▪ After all players have had a turn, (or after a set amount of time) the team with the most points wins.

Goals: Competition; increased activity; maintain and improve hand-eye coordination and communication

Adaptation: The size of the wire hoop and the position of the wastebasket may be adjusted according to the abilities of the players.

Beanbag Golf

Stages: One and Two

Location: Inside or outdoors—a great game to include any household children on a rainy day

Equipment: Golf club; beanbags; masking tape; paper and pencils for scoring

Description of Activity

▪ Mark off several five-inch squares on the floor or ground with masking tape to simulate a series of "holes" in a golf course.

▪ Using the golf club, each player tries to hit the beanbag into the marked squares with as few strokes as possible. The score for each "hole" is the number of strokes required until the beanbag lands within one of the squares. All shots should be from at least four feet from the hole. Any player who does not succeed in getting the beanbag into a square in ten tries may mark a score of 10 on his or her score pad and pass on to the next hole.

▪ The player with the lowest score is the winner.

Goals: Competition; individual accomplishment; group activity; arm and leg exercise; maintain and improve hand-eye coordination

Adaptation: The "course" may be marked with as few or as many squares as desired, depending on the ability of the persons participating.

Beanbag Relay

Stages: One through Three

Location: Inside or outdoors

Equipment: Two beanbags; two trash cans

Description of Activity

▪ Set the trash cans parallel to each other several feet from the starting line. Divide players into two equal-numbered teams.

▪ With one player standing behind another on each team, have the two teams line up side by side an equal distance from the trash cans. Give the first player on each team a beanbag. At the signal to begin play, the first player on each team leaves the starting line and places the beanbag in the trash can and then returns to his or her team and goes to the end of the line. As soon as the first player has returned, the second player leaves the starting line and retrieves the beanbag from the trash can and gives it to the third player. The second player goes to the end of the line, and the third player leaves the starting line and puts the beanbag in the trash can and then goes to the end of the line. The fourth player retrieves the beanbag, and play continues in this manner until the first player has again reached the head of the line.

■ The team whose first player returns first to the head of the line is the winner.

Goals: Competition; team spirit and communication; family activity and exercise

Adaptation: A baton or cut-off broomstick may be used instead of beanbags. A chair seat or other designated place may be used instead of trash cans. Any number of teams may participate in the relay.

Blackjack

Stages: One and Two

Location: Kitchen or anywhere a table can be set up

Equipment: Poker chips, pennies, quarters, or M&M's; deck of playing cards

Description of Activity
■ Each player gets fifteen chips (same color) but cannot bet more than two chips at a time.

▪ Bets must be placed before the deal.

▪ Dealer (usually the caregiver) deals one card facedown to each player, including the dealer, and one card faceup. To make the game a little easier, you may choose to deal all cards faceup, except for the dealer's hole card (or bottom card).

▪ Number cards count at face value, face cards are each worth 10, and aces are worth either 1 or 11.

▪ Players try to get the most points while staying at or below 21. (Players are playing against the dealer, not each other.)

▪ Starting on the left, dealer goes around the table asking each player if he or she wants a "hit"; these cards are dealt faceup.

▪ Players place bets on their turn. You may use poker chips or any other items such as pennies, quarters, or M&M's.

▪ As the dealer, you pay everyone who beats you. For example, you have 17 and stay: you pay anyone who has 18, 19, 20, or 21; if a player also has 17, you break even, or "push"; if a player has less than 17, you take the chips that have been bet.

▪ You pay chip-for-chip except for blackjack (any face card and an ace), which pays double.

▪ Games should last approximately forty-five minutes. At the end of allotted time, the player with the most chips or coins wins. Special treats could be added as prizes for the winner, such as a piece of chocolate, hand cream, scented paper, or anything that is especially meaningful to your loved one.

Goals: Competition; socialization; maintain and improve memory and restorative skills (remembering names of objects)

Adaptation: With more experienced players, you may choose to include splitting and doubling. Splitting is when you have two aces or face cards and you play them as separate hands. Doubling is when you have a face card or ace and you can double your bet and receive one card only.

Bowling

Stages: One through Three

Location: Inside or outdoors

Equipment: Rectangular table; ten large cups; two rubber balls; pencil and paper for scoring. A plastic bowling set may also be used.

Description of Activity

- Set up the tenpins (drink containers) in a triangle at one end of the table.
- Divide the players into two equal-numbered teams. The two teams line up on opposite sides of the table.
- Standing at the end of the table opposite the tenpins, the members of the two teams take turns throwing the rubber balls down the table to knock over as many tenpins as possible. Each player throws two balls per turn, and each player gets five turns. After every player has had five turns throwing the balls, the game ends.
- A score sheet is kept, and 1 point is scored for each pin that is knocked over, except that a player who knocks over all the pins on the first try is given 2 points for every pin, making a strike worth 20 points.

■ Players' individual points are totaled, and then the individual scores are added together to determine the team score. The team with the higher score wins.

Goals: Recreation; competition; teamwork; mild exercise; aid in developing orientation

Adaptation: The game may be played for highest individual score rather than a team score or may combine both. Instead of using a table, set up the pins on the floor in a long hallway to simulate a bowling alley.

Grasshopper

Stages: One and Two; Three and Four with hand–over–hand assistance

Location: Inside or outdoors

Equipment: Dice; paper and colored markers

Description of Activity
■ Distribute a sheet of paper, a pencil, and a die to each person. (One die may be shared among participants.)
■ The players throw a die to draw the body of a grasshopper as follows:

The player must first throw a 1 for the body of the grasshopper.
Next, the player must throw a 2 for the grasshopper's head.
Then, in any order, the player must throw two 3s, one for each of the grasshopper's antennae; two 4s, one for each of the grasshopper's eyes; one 5 for the grasshopper's mouth; and six 6s, one for

each of the grasshopper's legs. Using the paper and markers, the players draw whatever part of the grasshopper they rolled for.

- Only one throw of the die is allowed per player, per turn, unless the desired number is thrown. If the desired number is thrown, the player's turn continues and he or she may roll the die again. If a players rolls a number for a part that has already been drawn, the turn is forfeited and it is the next player's turn. It is helpful if the caregiver has a picture of a grasshopper on hand to serve as a visual aid.
- The first player to complete the grasshopper wins.

Goals: Sense of achievement; maintain and improve hand-eye coordination; improve concentration and memory; increase bonding and communication with caregiver

Adaptation: Any other animal may be used instead of a grasshopper.

Lucky Penny Game

Stages: One through Three

Location: Inside, in-room, or outdoors

Equipment: Large jar with lid; water; small jar without lid that can fit inside larger jar; carpenter's knife; pennies

Description of Activity
- Fill the large jar almost to the top with water. Place the small jar inside the large jar, submerged in water. With the carpenter's knife (found in any hardware store), cut a slit in the center of the

lid that is at least half the size of the lid. Open the slit some so that pennies can freely fall through it. Then screw the lid on the larger jar.

■ Players drop the pennies through the slit, trying to get them into the small jar inside.

Goals: Maintain and improve hand-eye coordination; excellent distraction tool—watching pennies fall through the water into the small jar holds people's interest

Adaptation: This can be played as either an individual game or a team game. Depending on the abilities of the players, it may be necessary to remove the lid from the jar.

Miss the Bell

Stages: One through Three

Location: Inside, in-room

Equipment: Small, soft ball; eight-inch embroidery hoops; small bell; string

Description of Activity

■ Place the bell on a piece of string about six to eight inches long. Secure the string between the two embroidery hoops so that the bell is suspended about three inches into the center of the hoop. Hang the hoop from a ceiling fixture or doorframe so that it is about eye level.

■ Standing about six feet away, players try to put the ball through the hoop without ringing the bell. One point is scored each time the ball goes through the hoop, and 3 points are scored each time the ball goes through the hoop without ringing the bell. You can adjust the distance from the hoop according to ability. Set a playing time of fifteen to thirty minutes.

Goals: Recreation; competition; group activity; exercise; maintain and improve hand-eye coordination

Adaptation: This game can be an excellent diversional activity for someone who is bed-bound.

Newspaper Tearing

Stages: One through Four

Location: Inside

Equipment: Newspapers

Description of Activity

- Assemble a large pile of newspapers in the work area.
- Give each person a section of newspaper. The caregiver names an object—such as a car—and the participants try to find a likeness of that object and tear it out. Then another object is named and the same procedure is followed. If more than one person is playing, such as family members, award points for the best likeness.
- Simple objects are best—such as a box, tree, moon, star, car, truck, football, doll, fish, tiger, horse, or other animal. This could be tailored to your loved one's special interest, such as gardening, sports, or fishing. Review the newspaper or magazine to

ensure the objects that are named are present (inability to find an object could lead to frustration).

■ The person with the most points at the end of the game is the winner. If only the loved one and the caregiver are involved, the torn pictures will provide an opportunity for congenial discussions and laughs.

Goals: Competition; mental stimulation; maintain and improve hand–eye coordination

Adaptation: While this activity can be used as a game, it can also be used on an individual basis as a creative project. Freehand drawings may be made of the objects instead of tearing paper.

Ping-Pong Football

Stages: One through Three

Location: Inside or outdoors

Equipment: Ping-Pong ball; card table or small dining table; masking tape; two sections of newspaper

Description of Activity

■ Fold newspaper into two tubes (one for each player) approximately eight by twelve inches.

■ Mark the center of the table with masking tape.

■ Place the Ping-Pong ball in the center of the table. Players stand at opposite ends. Using the folded newspaper, each player tries to fan the ball toward the opponent's side of the table. The opponent then tries to fan it back without allowing the ball to fall off the table.

- One point is scored each time the ball falls off the table. The first player to reach 10 points is the winner.
- You may wish to include gifts or prizes that can be shared. After a grueling game of Ping-Pong football, you can sit together and share the prize and the quality time.

Goals: Recreation; family activity; competition; exercise; maintain and improve hand-eye coordination

Adaptation: While this makes a good one-on-one game, more than two people can play it on a larger table.

Playing-Card Bingo

Stages: One through Three

Location: Anywhere a table can be set up—this is a great game to involve everyone in the house

Equipment: Two decks of playing cards

Description of Activity

- Deal an equal number of cards from the standard deck to each player.
- Players may arrange their cards any way they wish as long as they can see each card.
- The caller shuffles the large deck and then calls the top card.
- Whoever has the card called discards it in the middle of the table.

- The first player to discard all of his or her cards is the winner.
- If you like, you can play until one person is left; that person also wins.

Goals: Socialization; object recognition; maintain and improve memory and restorative skills (remembering names of objects)

Po-ke-no

Stages: One and Two

Location: Inside

Equipment: Po-ke-no boards; chips; deck of cards (Po-ke-no boards are made with decks of ordinary playing cards, sixteen cards to a board, with four cards in each direction)

Description of Activity

- Choose a caller and distribute a Po-ke-no board and chips to each player.
- The caller takes the first card from the deck, calls it out, and also shows it to the players. If the caller's card appears on a player's board, the player places a chip on that spot. Play continues in this manner. The first player to get four chips in a row is the winner. The row may be either vertical, horizontal, or diagonal.

Goals: Competition; concentration; sense of achievement; increase communication skills and activity; maintain and improve hand-eye coordination

Adaptation: Instead of standard Po-ke-no boards, any other pictures or cards may be substituted as long as the cards used by the caller match the cards on the boards used by the players. This is a great game to be creative and create a board based on cultural traditions.

Power of Observation Game

Stages: One and Two

Location: Inside or in room of bed-bound loved one

Equipment: Table or tray; cloth; twelve items of any kind, such as keys, hairbrush, comb, lotion, magnifying glass, or glasses

Description of Activity

- Place all of the items on a table.
- Let the participants observe what is on the table for fifteen to twenty seconds. Point to each item individually and name it. Then, cover the table with the cloth and remove one item, keeping it concealed. Uncover the table and see if the participants can remember which item is missing.
- Do this until you are down to three or four items. Each correct answer receives 1 point. Award a prize for a winning score —the most points if there are multiple participants or a set number of points if only one person is playing.

Goals: Develop skills in observation, recall, and memory; helpful for persons lacking orientation skills or who have had a stroke

Adaptation: This game can also be played in reverse. After playing by identifying the missing items, remove all items except two or three. Again allow the players to observe the items, and then cover them. Add items to the table one at a time and ask the participants to name the item that was just added. This game makes an excellent activity before or after lunch to increase bonding and communication between the caregiver and the person being cared for.

Sponge Game

Stages: One and Two (Stage Three with assistance)

Location: Inside, in-room, or outdoors

Equipment: Two wide, flat bowls; a sponge cut into spoon-size chunks; tablespoon; blindfold

Description of Activity

■ Place the sponge pieces in one of the bowls. Set the bowls next to each other on a table, about an inch apart.

■ The player stands in front of the bowls and is blindfolded. Using only the tablespoon, the player attempts to move the pieces of sponge from one bowl to the other within a set time limit—about thirty seconds usually works well. The player who moves the most pieces is the winner.

Goals: Hand coordination; competition; family interaction

Adaptation: According to the abilities of the participants, it may be helpful for the players to practice moving the sponge pieces first without the blindfold. Provides a great opportunity for smaller children to interact with the loved one and also is a good party game.

Tic-Tac-Toe

Stages: One through Three

Location: Inside, in-room, or outdoors

Equipment: One eight-inch square board, one inch thick; four large wooden thread spools; four one-by-one-inch square boards about two inches thick; enamel paint, at least four colors of your choice; bristle paint brushes

Description of Activity
- Paint the board a solid color and allow to dry until no longer tacky (approximately two hours). Using a different color, paint lines creating nine equal squares on the board.
- Paint the spools one color, and paint the wooden blocks another color.
- This game is played just as tic-tac-toe is always played, using the spools and wooden blocks for Xs and Os.

Goals: Maintain and improve concentration and hand-eye coordination; a good game for persons who cannot or will not generally participate in other activities, as the spools and wooden blocks are easier to handle than the usual pencil-and-paper version of tic-tac-toe

Adaptation: This is also a good game for children who lack writing skills and for people with arthritis.

Touch and Tell Game

Stages: One through Three

Location: Inside, in-room, or outdoors

Equipment: Basket; blindfold; assortment of objects—clothespin, thimble, hairpin, pencil, screwdriver, wrench, key, watch, and so forth

Description of Activity
- Place the items in the basket.
- Players are blindfolded and must try to identify the objects in the basket through touch.
- The player who is able to identify all of the objects in the shortest amount of time is the winner.

Goals: Mental stimulation; recreation; improve memory and restorative skills (remembering names of objects)

Adaptation: This is a good game for loved ones who have impaired vision or are bed-bound. Rather than using a blindfold, you can place the objects in a large box or paper bag with holes cut for the hands.

Wicker Ball

Stages: One and Two

Location: Inside, in-room, or outdoors

Equipment: Empty bleach bottles with handles, one for each player; small handsaw; masking tape; yarn ball (see "Pom-Poms/ Fuzz Balls" in Arts and Crafts chapter)

Description of Activity

- Cut bleach bottles in half with a small handsaw, retaining the top half with the handle, and cover the rough edges with masking tape (to avoid scratching). These serve as catch baskets.
- Each player holds a catch basket in one hand.
- Place the yarn ball inside one of the catch baskets. The player thrusts the basket forward and upward, throwing the yarn ball to another player, who reaches forward with his or her basket to catch the ball. Play continues in this manner.

Goals: Recreation; exercise; social interaction; maintain and improve hand-eye coordination

Adaptation: With more than two players, the game can be made competitive by eliminating those who miss the ball or by dividing the group into two teams, allowing each team to score a point if the other team misses the ball. People in wheelchairs or geriatric chairs can also participate.

Gardening

Gardening, as a pastime, is widely enjoyed today in all cultures, but it may have special significance to elderly people in our society who were reared in a time when the country was predominately rural and almost everyone enjoyed some type of gardening. In addition, caring for plants is a personal activity that provides an outlet for people's nurturing instinct. There are many ways that people with varying interests and abilities can enjoy gardening, from having a potted plant in a window to maintaining a large vegetable or flower garden. People in Stages One and Two may enjoy monthly garden club meetings. Many local garden clubs welcome the opportunity to give lectures, present demonstrations, and display various flower and vegetable growing techniques.

Ideas

- High school agriculture clubs (such as Future Farmers of America and 4-H) and classes are sources of volunteers to assist with vegetable gardening. Colleges and universities also have agriculture departments that will provide consultation and assistance.
- Local garden clubs and rose societies will assist with planning and executing gardens.
- Loved ones can start small plants in decorative pots to give as gifts or as a group project to sell in bazaars. Miniature roses are easily grown in pots on patios and sunny locations indoors.
- African violets are ideal for bedside plants, as they are small, easy to grow, and do well in artificial light.
- Many people enjoy planting bulbs in flower beds or pots in the fall. Nurseries will often donate plants at the season's end.
- Window boxes are rewarding and attractive. Able persons can construct and paint simple boxes. Bed-bound family members can also participate in gardening by transplanting a potted plant from a window box to a bedside table for a loved one to water, feed, and prune. (See "Window Boxes" later in this chapter.)
- A large vegetable or flower garden can be enjoyed as a family project.
- If you can accommodate a large group, you can invite garden clubs, rose societies, and African violet societies to hold meetings in your home.
- A loved one who is interested in gardening should be encouraged to join gardening groups, and efforts should

be made to arrange transportation to meetings and special events such as tours of gardens. Encourage the loved one to enter flowers and plants in shows, county fairs, and other exhibitions, and be sure to display any ribbons or awards.

Goals: Sense of accomplishment; maintain and improve socialization skills; acquire new skills; aid memory; enjoy the simple pleasure of watching something grow; also provides a great way to involve the whole family

Bonsai Crazy

Bonsai miniature gardening has been practiced for centuries in China and Japan. Bonsai is the reproduction of natural tree forms in miniature. It is a beautiful form of gardening that can be performed indoors as well as outdoors in fair weather. Although they do require quite a bit of maintenance, they can provide hours of enjoyment and a sense of accomplishment. Many types are on the market; check local gardening suppliers for the nearest distributor of bonsai materials.

Stages: One through Three; Four with hands-on assistance

Location: Indoors or outside

Equipment: Shallow rectangular ceramic dish planter with drainage holes (special bonsai planters are available); a small piece of screen; two to three bonsai plants; bonsai soil (mixture of equal parts conifer mix, tropical, and subtropical potting soils);

mister or spray bottle; pebbles; florist or bonsai wire; bonsai wire cutter

Description of Activity

■ Place screen over drainage holes in planter to prevent soil escaping during watering.

■ Fill planter with mixture of soil and place at least two plants in desired location. Keep in mind that the bonsai arrangement should mirror a natural setting. Lightly tap the soil around the plants to secure them in the soil.

■ Bend the wire around the branches tautly—but not tight—into the desired position. Snip off excess wire with bonsai cutters. Do not use regular wire cutters or pliers because this will damage the delicate nature of the plants.

■ Decorate the top of the soil using pebbles, rocks, or small ceramic animals to reflect a nature scene.

■ Place plant in filtered sunlight and mist daily. The soil should be moist but not wet.

Goals: Provide relaxation and a sense of accomplishment; maintain hand-eye coordination.

Adaptation: Bonsai can be a group activity involving the whole family. This is also a fantastic activity for bed-bound people, providing them with hours of beauty and an avenue for solo activity. These also make excellent gifts and bazaar items.

Potted Rose Garden

Not everyone has room for a rose garden, but if you and the one you care for love roses, take heart—you can surround yourself with container roses.

Stages: Stages One through Four

Location: Outdoors

Equipment: Selection of roses; several pots at least eighteen inches deep (twelve inches for miniature roses) with a twelve-inch diameter; pebbles; loam-based potting soil; bone meal or rose fertilizer; gardening gloves

Description of Activity

- First choose containers. You will need one for each rose plant.
- When choosing your container, put some thought into your selection—roses live for quite a while and you will want a pot that is equal in beauty to your roses.
- Talk to your local gardening club or supplier for tips on which roses do best in your area. This is also a great time to involve your loved one. Spend some time reviewing pictures of the appropriate roses and let them pick the color scheme.
- When you are ready to plant your rosebushes, line the bottom of the containers with pebbles or gravel to ensure proper drainage (usually about one inch); fill the rest of the pot with loam-based soil.
- Using your hands, dig a hole and place the rosebush in the center of the container with the top of the root ball an inch below the top of the container. This will prevent water from spilling over during watering. Fill the space around the root ball

with the potting soil and tap down lightly. Be sure to cover the root ball completely. Immediately water the rose bush.

■ Place the containers where the roses will get at least five hours of sun a day. Water daily in the summer during the hottest part of the day and give the plants a yearly boost with bone meal or rose fertilizer. (Talk to your garden supplier for tips on when it is appropriate and the amount for your area.)

■ Monitor loved ones very carefully to ensure they do not put soil, bone meal, or fertilizer in their mouths.

■ For an added personal touch, pots can be hand-painted.

Goals: Improve and maintain fine motor skills; improve and maintain hand-eye coordination; teach new skills and aid in memory retention (you must water frequently); provide an avenue for a sense of accomplishment and the enjoyment of watching something grow. Planting is an excellent distraction activity. The whole family, including young ones, can get involved.

Adaptation: Gardening in containers can offer boundless possibilities for cleverly decorating small areas indoors as well as outdoors. Check with your local gardening supplier for tips on nonpoisonous houseplants and appropriate containers and pots.

Temperamental Terrariums

Terrariums are great for growing small houseplants and carnivorous plants. Small houseplants (two to four inches tall) can be grown in almost any glass container. One-and-a-half-gallon fishbowls are an excellent choice. The container can also be as large as a two-hundred-gallon fish tank. Terrariums do take some skill, so I would recommend that you start out with a small one-gallon fishbowl or tank before moving on to something larger. Remember to choose only plants that are nontoxic if ingested. Exotic plants such as orchids can be grown indoors.

Stages: One through Three; Four with hands-on assistance

Location: Indoors or outside

Equipment: One-and-a-half- to three-gallon fishbowl; mild soap and paper towels; pebbles; tropical planting soil (enough to fill at least four inches of the bowl); several nontoxic houseplants (two to four inches tall); spray bottle or mister, small ceramic items, rocks for decorating

Description of Activity

■ Cleanse fishbowl with a mild soap and water, rinse well and dry with paper towel.

■ Place approximately one inch of pebbles at the bottom of the fishbowl; fill with four inches of soil.

■ Place the selected plants in the soil. Cover with a small amount of additional soil and lightly tap soil to secure plants.

■ Decorate area around plants with pebbles, small ceramic items, or small rocks

■ Lightly water and mist daily. Place in area with diffused light.

A Word About Carnivorous Plants: While they can be an interesting focal point for conversation, carnivorous plants will need special care.

- Do not top water. Give small amount of water and let it dribble down the side of the bowl, not directly on the plant. Always use bottled water.
- Do not force-feed the plant. They will actually be able to catch enough insects on their own.
- Do not fertilize.
- Do not use potting soil. Use a mixture of 60 percent peat moss and 40 percent white perlite.
- Keep out of direct sunlight.

Goals: Excellent source of hands-on activities; provide a sense of accomplishment and provide an outlet for a nurturing nature; can be a very interesting conversational piece

Window Boxes

Window boxes are an excellent addition to the small garden and can be added to almost any window. A variety of kits are available at garden supply stores. Window boxes can also be customized or painted to match your house, or decorated by the person you are caring for to match his or her interests. It makes an excellent source of entertainment for anyone who is bedbound.

Location: Outdoors

Equipment: Window box to match the window's dimensions; potting soil (enough to fill within one inch of the top); selected plants; paints and decorations if desired

Description of Activity

- Decorate window box as desired.
- Attach to window per manufacturer's instructions.
- Fill box with potting soil and water completely (until all soil is moist).
- Dig a hole with your hands and insert the selected flower or plant. Cover the roots with soil and lightly tap soil to secure the plant in place. Repeat until all plants are in the box. Be sure to allow enough room between each plant, based on the kind of plant or flower you choose.
- Flowers can be selected according to the desired outcome— for example, constant bloom or butterfly or bird attraction.
- Water daily.

Goals: Provide a sense of accomplishment, relaxation, and the pleasure of not only watching something grow but the beauty of the finished product

Grooming

Just a few words about grooming—"It can be a nightmare!" It is common for elderly people to balk at taking a bath and maintaining healthy grooming habits. There are valid reasons for this reluctance. One of the most important is fear. They are afraid of falling, breaking bones, or getting chilled (for elderly people, a common cold can be life threatening). Combing hair becomes painful with arthritis, and many times other grooming habits can cause discomfort and pain as well. Brushing teeth can hurt if the person has caries. The skin may be overly sensitive and hurt when rubbed with lotion.

There are also many medical reasons for not wanting to bathe. Depression, which is common in the elderly, may cause lack of interest in personal hygiene. Elderly people also tire more easily and may not feel like they have the energy to bathe and maintain proper hygiene. Of course, with those who suffer from Alzheimer's and other dementias, distraction is always a problem.

They may start a project, such as combing their hair, and become distracted and never finish. However, with patience and the appropriate techniques, proper hygiene can be maintained, and grooming can be an enjoyable experience for both you and your loved one.

Ideas

- Time will vary according to the procedure; watch for signs that the person has lost interest or patience.
- If you see that your loved one becomes overly tired, bathe before bedtime.
- Make sure to explain each activity being performed before starting it to reduce any anxiety the loved one may experience.
- Take special care when using clippers and other sharp items.
- Remember that items used by more than one person must be cleaned between uses.
- Liven things up with music—for example, play a barbershop quartet when clipping a man's hair.
- Provide praise and compliments.
- Make sure to warm the bathroom and towels prior to use.
- Lotion and moist towelets can be warmed in the microwave for a few seconds.
- A long, absorbent, terrycloth robe will decrease drying time.
- Purchase soap on a rope to prevent accidental falls.
- Replace difficult twist tops with pump dispensers.

- Install grab bars in shower and bath to minimize risk of falls.
- Electric toothbrushes make brushing teeth easier.
- Use pump toothpaste.
- Use only hypoallergic toiletries.
- Make sure the bathroom floor has nonskid stripping (found at any department store).
- Use the loved one's favorite scent after bathing or mix a little with the liquid soap.
- Use nontearing shampoo and body wash.
- Use a detangler when washing hair and a large-toothed comb to prevent pulling on hair.
- Give a quick foot massage after bathing to promote circulation, assess condition of feet, and provide relaxation.
- Make it a special occasion—use the time to bond with your loved one.

Daily Grooming

Many times a sponge bath can be taken in place of a full bath or shower and it is a lot less taxing. Daily grooming is not meant to completely replace a bath, but it will help on those days when your loved one does not want to take a bath.

Stages: One through Four

Location: Inside

Equipment: Table and chairs; sink; washbasin; full-length mirror and large hand mirror; towels, washcloths, and soap; plastic caddy to hold grooming items (toothbrush, toothpaste, shampoo, nail files, razors, deodorant, etc.)

Description of Activity

▪ Make sure all required articles are in the designated area. After breakfast and any morning medications, take the loved one to the area.

▪ Fill the washbasin with warm water and give the person a towel, a washcloth, and soap. Start by having the person wash their face and hands. Because everyone works at a different speed, never hurry people for whom you're caring. Allow them to finish at their own speed.

▪ Next, ask loved ones to locate their toothbrush and toothpaste. Then ask them to brush their teeth and rinse their mouth. People who are unable to get up to the sink should be given a basin for this purpose.

▪ Assist those with dentures with rinsing and applying denture fixative to the dentures before placing in their mouth. Monitor for proper fit and assess gums for any red or swollen areas. If there is swelling or redness, the loved one should see a dentist as soon as possible.

▪ Next ask them to identify their hairbrush and comb to fix their hair. Monitor any hairpieces for cleanliness and assist when needed on proper placement. Wigs and toupes made from human hair can be cleaned and set like normal hair. Synthetic hair should be done by a professional.

▪ Ask the men to shave, and assist if needed. Women can be assisted with shaving underarms and legs if desired. However, as women age, most hair in these areas is very fine and sparse and may not require frequent shaving.

- When time permits, ask the one you are caring for to assist in cleaning the nails.
- Keep in mind that you may have to offer assistance with any of these tasks.

Bathing

- Always provide adequate privacy; many people are very modest about having someone see their bodies. Although, you may have to stand by or actually assist with the bathing, keep your loved one's privacy in mind. Make sure all doors are shut, and only have the person's body visible when needed.
- Floors around tub and shower areas should have nonskid strips.
- Have two basins, one with warm soapy water and the other with clear warm water. Use nontear body soap.
- Using a washcloth, gently wash feet and legs. Use clean washcloths dipped in plain water to rinse. Wrap each leg in a warm towel.
- Wash abdomen and chest using the same technique as above and cover with a towel.
- Next, wash hands and arms; remove towels from legs and wrap arms.
- Using a clean washcloth, gently wash eyes from inside to out and then facial areas and ears. Rinse and dry with a warm towel.
- Cleanse the perineal areas with warm soapy water, then rinse and dry with a warm towel.
- Discard water.
- Apply lotion from feet to facial features, keeping areas covered with a warm towel until ready to dress.
- Before the loved takes a bath or shower, it may be necessary to heat up the room and warm the towels in the dryer or

microwave. Always make sure the water temperature is comfortable. Assure loved ones that you will stand by to help and protect them from falling.

■ Shower chairs can be a big help in providing security for loved ones. Since they are able to sit in the chair in the shower, it reduces the fear of slipping. Always assist to a standing or sitting position.

■ Make sure to wash and rinse hair completely with a nontearing shampoo. Wrap hair with a warm towel immediately after bathing. You may also use a "dry shampoo," which does not need to be rinsed out. This can be bought at most department stores or medical supply stores. This type of shampoo is applied to the hair and, after drying, is simply brushed out.

■ Assist with dressing as needed in the warm bathroom.

Goals: Increase pride in appearance; improve self-esteem, body image, direction-following skills, and error recognition

Adaptation: An evaluation of your loved one's grooming skills is very helpful. It is a good idea to do the evaluation the first week and then update it every three or four months. Your loved one may also enjoy a day at the hairdresser's, which could be incorporated into a community outing. Many hairstylists will provide in-home services as well; call your favorite barber or salon to inquire.

Manicure

Stages: One through Four

Location: Inside

Equipment: Hand towels; small margarine cup; liquid dish detergent; orange sticks; nail scissors or clippers; cuticle remover; cotton balls; emery boards; hand cream; rubbing alcohol; non-acetone nail polish remover; nail buffer; nail polish (clear for men, color of choice for women)

Description of Activity

- Seat the person at a table with a mirror.
- Place warm water and a little detergent in the margarine cup, and soak the fingers for about two minutes.
- Take one hand out of the water, and leave the other to soak.
- Remove any old nail polish with the non-acetone remover. Repeat for other hand, then discard water.
- Clean under the nails with an orange stick.
- Clip the nails.
- Dab on cuticle remover, and push the cuticles back with an orange stick covered in a little cotton.
- Smooth any rough edges with an emery board.
- Apply cream to the hands and forearms.
- Clean the tops of the nails with cotton soaked in a little alcohol.
- Buff the nails and apply polish as desired.

Pedicure

Foot care is extremely important for elderly people. Open sores must be treated immediately for people with diabetes. Often foot discoloration and swelling is the first sign of other serious health problems. Contact a physician regarding any changes in your loved one's feet.

Because most elderly people have arthritis to a certain degree, having a pedicure may be a painful process. You can make it easier by providing warm towels, supporting the legs when raised, and having an easy touch. Making it a special occasion always helps generate enthusiasm, so make a big deal out it. Make the loved one feel like a queen or king for the day.

Stages: One through Three

Location: Inside

Equipment: Large basin, mild soap, such as baby shampoo, Ivory, or baby body wash, and warm water; Turkish towels or similar soft towels, warmed; non-acetone nail polish remover; cuticle remover; orange sticks; cotton balls; nail scissors or clippers; emery boards; lotion; rubbing alcohol; nail polish

Description of Activity

▪ Fill basin with warm water until three inches from the top. Mix one teaspoon of baby shampoo or other mild soap in the water.

▪ Be sure to place a towel under the basin to absorb any spills.

▪ Soak feet in warm, soapy water for approximately fifteen minutes.

▪ Sitting in front of your loved one, remove one foot from the water and wrap it in a warm towel.

- Remove any old polish and apply cuticle cream.
- Gently clean under the nails with an orange stick; then, with a small amount of cotton on the tip, push back the cuticles.
- Clip the nails, and smooth with an emery board.
- Return the foot to the water and repeat the steps with the other foot.
- Remove both feet from the water and dry them.
- Apply warm lotion with a massaging motion to feet and calves.
- Clean the tops of the nails with cotton soaked in a little alcohol.
- Buff the nails and apply polish as desired.
- Any corn or callus treatment should be addressed by a licensed podiatrist.

Goals: Maintain and improve hygiene of feet; improve self-image; encourage assistance in personal grooming; help monitor changes in health

Makeup and Beauty

Getting dressed up and applying makeup has been a cornerstone to feeling beautiful in many women's eyes. This can be a great time before an outing to relax and relieve tension or it can just be a fun way to spend a visit when there is nothing else to do. It makes a great time for sharing memories of proms and special nights out.

Stages: One through Four

Location: Inside

Equipment: Lotion; makeup sponges; foundation; loose powder; eye shadow with brushes; blush and blush brush; eyebrow pencil; mascara. Always use hypoallergenic makeup products.

Description of Activity

- Start with a nice clean face.
- Choose a shade of liquid foundation closest to your loved one's natural color.
- Using a makeup sponge or your fingers, dab a small amount on chin, cheeks, and forehead, and under eyes.
- Next, blend the foundation using gentle upward strokes until completely blended. This can be done with the pads of your fingers or a makeup sponge. Check carefully around hairline and chin for streaks or lines.
- Using the loose powder, lightly powder your loved one's face.
- Be careful not to get powder in the eyes or mouth.
- The next step is applying a small amount of blush with a blush brush to each cheekbone. Carefully blend blush along cheek. The color should stay within the peaches and be just dark enough to add dimension. Stay away from heavy red and plums, as these tend to wash out elderly skin. For darker skin, use browns and rusts.
- Now add the eye shadow of your choice. For a professional look, apply a lighter shade to the brow bone and the lid of the eye, and then blend a darker shade in the crease. This opens the eye and brightens the color of the eyes.
- If your loved one has faint eyebrows, you can fill them in with an eyebrow pencil. Using small short strokes, apply brow pencil to the eyebrows. Never draw on eyebrows—just use light strokes to fill in. Stay away from black or dark browns. Normally, a light brown is suitable for all people.

■ Mascara may also be added, if desired. Have the person look down, and using light upward stokes, apply the mascara from the bottom of the lash to the end. Next, have the person look up and apply in the same manner to the bottom lashes. Mascara can be difficult to remove, so you may wish to purchase eye makeup remover as well. Always use hypoallergenic products.

Goals: Improve self-image; increase socialization skills; increase interest in hygiene

Adaptation: You can also include a picture day. Put on dress clothes and, after applying makeup, take snapshots and give to friends. This could also be a nice addition after having hair styled either at home or by a professional. Please note that a professional should do any hair coloring. Injury to the eyes by the hair color or damage to the hair by using a too-strong product or combinations of hair dye and medication that is currently being taken is always a possibility with any home application.

Music

The ability of music to influence behavior is recognized universally. Music can encourage socialization, bring joy, soothe, cheer, and evoke fantasy, as well as encourage self-expression and communication. The possible applications for music are almost limitless, and the potential value to the individual is great. Fortunate is the person who possesses musical talent; however, lack of musical ability does not prevent the use of music in activities. The positive value of music in an activity relates to the psychological and emotional response of the participants and does not depend on excellence of performance or high standards of achievement.

Musical activities can be either active or passive, and a well-planned program provides opportunities to enjoy music through active participation as well as passive listening. Music need not be limited to any certain type and can include classical, folk, popular, religious, vocal, instrumental, and many more styles, with selections based on a person's preference and enjoyment. Encourage people who sing or play instruments to do so. Some people enjoy performing for family and friends, whereas others are inhibited by an audience or simply enjoy playing alone. Do not require people to perform for others; however, do express appreciation when people share their talents, even if the effort was less than perfect. The use of radios, stereos, CD players, and so forth is also recommended.

Ideas

- Sing-alongs using simple old standards are always well received.
- Feel free to be spontaneous with your singing. Just the two of you can enjoy a song together. Including songs you learned when you were a kid will invite pleasant memories for both of you.
- If your loved one can play the piano or guitar, encourage him or her to accompany sing-alongs.
- Encourage someone who enjoys singing to lead the group.
- Encourage your loved one to sing along with musical recordings.
- Play musical games that involve naming a tune, remembering lyrics to popular music of previous eras, or improvising lyrics to music.
- Build tape or record libraries of seasonal and special-occasion songs and music. Ask your loved one which songs he or she would like to include.
- Consider music boxes for bedside tables.

- Invite music teachers to hold recitals for people who feel uncomfortable in crowded areas.
- Having a pianist, violinist, or guitarist play during mealtimes—or playing recorded music—can make the occasion more pleasant. Often, musicians will donate their time.
- College towns often provide access to choral groups, advanced recitals in many instruments, string groups, orchestras, bands, and vocalists. Invite talented people to perform at your home.
- Invite church choirs to sing in your home or hold rehearsals there.
- Recruit volunteers who will not only perform for your loved one but also offer instruction on how to play instruments.
- Following a musical performance, ask the musicians to demonstrate how to use their instruments.
- Bell choirs can perform for your loved one and assist him or her in giving it a try.
- Invite local instrument makers to give a brief workshop on their craft. Even piano tuners can demonstrate their work.
- Remember that whistling, clapping, toe tapping, and similar actions are valid musical expressions.

Rhythm Band

Stages: One through Four

Location: Inside or outdoors

Equipment: Records, cassettes, and/or CDs; songbooks; sheet music; various musical instruments (see "Rhythm Band Instruments" in the Arts and Crafts chapter)

Description of Activity

- Invite friends and family members to participate.
- Change records as necessary and bang on instruments to the beat.

Goals: Physical activity; enjoyment of music; relaxation; maintain and improve hand-eye coordination and socialization skills

Name That Tune

Music can be a great source of relaxation for many. It also inspires and brings back childhood and early adult memories. Playing Name That Tune is an excellent way to introduce reminiscence activities. Music soothes and relaxes and allows the loved one and the person caring for them a time for bonding. Of course, everyone is encouraged to sing along.

Stages: One and Two; Stages Three and Four may not be able to name the tune but will enjoy listening

Location: Inside or outdoors

Equipment: Record player; cassette player or CD player, selection of songs

Description of Activity

▪ Select a variety of tunes from the era that the one you are caring for is interested in (usually the years they were twenty to forty years of age).

▪ Play one tune at a time. The first person to guess the name of the song gets awarded 1 point.

▪ You can set a time limit of thirty minutes and the one who has the most points wins, or set a score amount such as 10 points and the first one to get the points is the winner.

Goals: Provide a relaxing time; increase socialization skills; provide avenue for reminiscence; increase or maintain memory capabilities

Music and a Story

Stages: One through Four

Location: Inside or outdoors

Equipment: Record player; CD player; cassette

Description of Activity

▪ Ask the loved one to pick out a few of his or her favorite songs. You can also get lists of oldies but goodies from your local music store and let the one you are caring for look at the list and circle his or her favorite songs.

■ For each song played the person must share a memory associated with the song or tell what they like about the song. You and your loved one can take turns telling stories.

■ Set at least thirty minutes to an hour for some special times to share this music with your loved one.

Goals: Provide increased socialization; maintain memory capabilities; provide reminiscence, relaxation, and opportunity for bonding

Name That Instrument

Almost everyone knows some types of musical instruments. They may not know how to play, but they do know what they look like and their names. This game is to enhance what is already known and provide an opportunity to learn something different.

Stages: One and Two

Location: Inside or outdoors

Equipment: Pictures of different musical instruments

Description of Activity

■ Show a picture of an instrument and give a brief explanation of the instrument (for example, makes high notes and sounds like a bird's song, while showing a picture of a flute). You can find a variety of pictures on the Internet or in books and magazines from a music store.

■ Each person who correctly identifies the instrument is awarded 1 point. The first one to reach 15 points is the winner.
■ You can award prizes or give a certificate of achievement to enhance enjoyment.

Goals: Provide memory enhancement; increase socialization skills; provide an avenue for enhanced learning of new information

Adaptation: Instruments can be chosen according the person's ethnic background as well. Note: If the game is too difficult or the person seems agitated, discontinue play and pick a different game.

Although many musical items can be found in the Arts and Crafts chapter, here are a few additional ones that might be fun to make and use.

Native American Rattle

Stages: One and Two; Three and Four with hands-on assistance

Location: Inside or outdoors

Equipment: One Y-shaped twig; yarn; scissors; tape; feathers; beads; buttons or shells with holes in them

Description of Activity
■ Hold the twig in one hand (descending part of twig should be long enough to hold comfortably).

■ Begin by wrapping the yarn around one prong of the Y. Secure yarn with a knot, or a piece of tape if the loved one does not have the dexterity to tie knots.

■ String beads, buttons, shells, or feathers along the way, and cover the yarn entirely. Knot or tape the end.

■ Start a new piece of yarn and tie to one end of the twig, stretching it across the Y-shape. String feathers, beads, and shells along the yarn and secure the yarn to the other prong of the Y. When shaken, it will make a rattling sound.

Goals: Provide a sense of accomplishment; improve or maintain hand-eye coordination; provide relaxation. This is a great distraction activity, and when younger members of the family join in, it increases socialization skills.

Maracas

A maraca is a Latin American and Tupi Indian rattle. The originals were made from hollow gourds filled with pebbles or seeds. These maracas are simple renditions made from paper plates. They are fun to make and are a great addition to the rhythm band. They are easy to use and make a delightful sound.

Stages: One and Two; Three and Four with hands-on assistance

Location: Inside or outdoors

Equipment: Two paper plates; colored markers or crayons; stapler; crepe paper streamers; dried beans, rice, or popcorn kernels

Description of Activity

- Decorate paper plates with crayons or colored markers.
- Staple long crepe paper streamers to the inside of the plate.
- Put a handful of dried beans, rice, or popcorn kernels in the paper plate.
- Place a paper plate on top of the other paper plate and staple all the way around. You can also make maracas with just one paper plate by folding it in half and stapling it shut.

Goals: Provide a sense of accomplishment; increase or maintain hand-eye coordination; provide opportunity for increased socialization

Rhythm and Rhyme

Although these may seem like childish rhymes, they are quite well-known and well-liked by the elderly. Remembering old rhymes and songs can be a nice distraction, and they make a nice addition to any activity. The rhymes and songs will bring back old memories of childhood or of singing them to their young children. They are a sure bet to bring a smile.

Stages: One through Four

Location: Inside or outdoors

Equipment: Tapes of old rhymes or sheet music; words or lyrics

Description of Activity

- Pass out papers with the words to the rhymes typed in large bold letters. You may need to assist the visually impaired.

- Begin singing and encourage others to sing along.
- The words to some old favorites are provided here.

Fiddle De Dee

> **Fiddle de dee, fiddle de dee,**
> **The fly has married the bumblebee.**
> **Said the fly, said he,**
> **"Will you marry me,**
> **and live with me, sweet bumblebee?"**
> **Fiddle de dee, fiddle de dee,**
> **The fly has married the bumblebee.**

Ride a Cockhorse to Banbury Cross

> **Ride a cockhorse to Banbury Cross**
> **To see a fine lady upon a white horse.**
> **Rings on her fingers, and bells on her toes.**
> **She shall have music wherever she goes.**

Old King Cole

> **Old King Cole was a merry old soul,**
> **And a merry old soul was he.**
> **He called for his pipe, and he called for his bowl,**
> **And he called for his fiddlers three.**
> **And every fiddler had a fiddle**
> **and a very fine fiddle had he.**
> **Oh there's none so rare, as can compare,**
> **With King Cole and his fiddlers three.**

Yankee Doodle

> **Yankee Doodle came to town,**
> **Riding on a pony,**
> **Stuck a feather in his hat**

And called it macaroni.
Yankee Doodle keep it up,
Yankee Doodle dandy,
Mind the music and the steps
And with the girls be handy.

Father and I went to camp,
Along with Captain Gooding,
and there we saw the men and boys,
As thick as hasty pudding.
Yankee Doodle keep it up,
Yankee Doodle dandy,
Mind the music and the steps,
And with the girls be handy.

Sing a Song of Sixpence

Sing a song of sixpence,
A pocket full of rye;
Four and twenty blackbirds,
Baked in a pie.
When the pie was opened
The birds began to sing;
Wasn't that a dainty dish
To set before the king?
The king was in the counting house,
Counting out his money.
The queen was in the parlor,
Eating bread and honey.
The maid was in the garden,
Hanging out the clothes;

When down came a blackbird
and snapped off her nose.

Goals: Enhance memory capabilities; provide opportunity for reminiscence, relaxation, and fun. It is also fun to do with the younger children in the home, increasing social skills for all participants.

Reality Orientation

Reality orientation is a therapeutic approach used to assist older adults who are disoriented from any cause—organic, physical, or emotional—by promoting their awareness of daily living factors in their immediate environment. The purpose is to help people develop and/or maintain interactions with their surroundings, peers, and caregivers in the most meaningful way.

Reality orientation brings information to your loved one regarding time, place, persons, and things in a way they can understand and incorporate into their daily life. The activities help them to determine where they are, who they are, what surrounds them, and what their responsibilities are. This awareness assists them in interacting with their surroundings in a meaningful, productive manner.

In its approach, reality orientation uses many principal treatments to provide appropriate care in challenging the aging process. However, a licensed therapist should enact many of these treatments, so we will be discussing only the areas appropriate for use in the home.

A direct result of an effective reality orientation is remotivation. The activities and strategies are designed to establish a direction for everyday living. Since many older people demonstrate a lack of interest in participating in organized activities, whether vocational or social, remotivation becomes an important consideration.

Reality orientation is an ongoing process of supplying information, correcting disoriented information, and reinforcing behaviors that approximate or reflect meaningful interactions with the individual's environment.

Treatment Techniques and Methodology

Reality orientation offers a variety of treatment techniques to the individual caregiver to assist the older person in managing and overcoming these impairments.

Ongoing Orientation

In an intensive form of reality orientation, current and personal information is presented and reviewed with the loved one on an ongoing basis. The caregiver also initiates discussions on a variety of subjects related to the person's interests. The caregiver's main objective is to improve the individual's ability to identify information regarding person (how we view information about ourselves and others), time (the year, time of day, season), and place (how we view information about where we are—home, hospital, city, state) and act on it appropriately. Reinforcing correct responses and repetition of information is highly recommended.

Instructional aids such as a felt board or chalkboard, large calendars and clocks, mailboxes, and in-and-out boards are utilized with the person's interest. The large felt boards or chalkboards are used to apply the day of the week, the season, the date, and any other pertinent information that the person needs to be reminded of. Pictures of people and their names can also be applied to aid in remembering. In-and-out boards are different types of closures, such as zippers, Velcro closures, snaps, and different types of locks attached to plywood. This aids in hand-eye coordination and retaining basic memory of how things work.

"Twenty-Four-Hour" Reality Orientation

This method requires the cooperation of every family member or other person who comes into contact with the individual. A joint effort is made to improve the individual's awareness and interaction in all activities in which he or she is engaged. It is recommended that all activities be verbally labeled. Correction and reinforcement are used consistently.

The "twenty-four-hour" reality orientation also requires that everyone involved with the individual share information and strategies. This effort can help assure carryover and increase results.

Special consideration is given to the "dependency syndrome." In this state, the individual's condition—disorientation, confusion, helplessness—is inadvertently reinforced by the caregiver and/or family members, who begin to take full custodial care of the person's needs, thereby moving the individual to a withdrawal state of dependency. When people ultimately expect nothing of the individual, the individual expects nothing of him- or herself. Memory and awareness are no longer needed, and like unexercised muscles, these faculties deteriorate. When caring for someone at home, you need to be aware of this possibility. It is easy to fall into doing everything for the person for whom you're caring, which only increases the level of dependency on you—and leads to caregiver burnout. Caregiver burnout can prevent you from providing adequate care.

Sensory Retraining Therapy

Sensory retraining therapy research indicates that all organisms need a certain minimum degree of stimulation—visual, auditory, tactile, and kinesthetic—to maintain normal, intelligent, adaptive behavior.

Sensory retraining therapy is designed for use with regressed older people who have a limited ability to interact with their environment. This treatment provides structured group and individual experiences aimed at all five senses. Each sense— sight, touch, taste, smell, and hearing—is discussed, and an activity is presented to accentuate it.

These activities, employing a variety of objects, are meant to stimulate the individual senses on a routine basis to maintain their functional use in the person's daily life. For example, colorful objects stimulate the eyes; sharp-smelling substances are contrasted with sweet-smelling substances to exercise the sense of smell; recordings of sounds of nature, playing musical instruments, and whispering provide a variety of auditory input; candy, pickles, and potato chips demonstrate different types of taste; soft versus hard, smooth versus rough, and hot versus cold items offer touch stimulation.

Resocialization

Resocialization uses specific techniques to stress interpersonal relations. The program offers geriatric participants an opportunity to be part of an accepting group—through the caregiver—and to give of themselves. By focusing on simple objective features of everyday life, not on factors related to personal emotional difficulties, the individual can establish fresh relationships and form friendships.

When the reality orientation program for older people was first implemented for long-term care facilities, it was not uncommon for participants to be unfamiliar with each other's names and even unconcerned with the person next to them. Members of the group seemed to be extremely self-centered, interested only in satisfying their own basic needs. However, as the group developed, a sense of "family" gradually occurred among members. Structured activities were presented to foster this attitude. For example, when a member of the group was absent due to an extended illness, each member was asked to make a get-well card for the person. By following the examples set by these types of programs, caregivers can help to establish this type of relationship with the individuals under their charge.

The program can help older people retain or regain their desire to live by exposing them regularly to the kind of experiences that give anyone the feeling that life is worthwhile. These shared experiences can produce lines of communication and interactions from individuals who have experienced deprivation and/or isolation in their lives. Resocialization has direct applications to persons living with Alzheimer's or dementia, who often isolate themselves because of their decreased functioning abilities.

It is important that the focus be on the relationship between the caregiver and the person being cared for; past unacceptable socialization patterns should be ignored. A fresh start is emphasized to encourage new acceptable relations within the milieu of the caregiver and the individual. Caregivers, as leaders, provide a model for behavior through their actions, acceptance, nonevaluative comments, and ability to raise questions. The resocialization activities establish an atmosphere of acceptance and freedom of expression whereby the person is enabled to discuss daily living concerns and happy experiences that otherwise might be overlooked.

All the activities within the book have been geared toward the act of resocialization of the person under your care. The activities are designed to assist the person to build trust with the caregiver, and many have a goal of increased socialization. Spending time with your loved one throughout the daily care in a nonjudgmental way, demonstrating patience and caring, will allow the loved one the opportunity to trust not only the caregiver but begin to open up to others as well. (See the chapter Socialization Activities for more on this topic.)

Breaking the Cycle of Dependency

The reality orientation activities are based on a therapeutic approach to assisting individuals who are exhibiting behaviors considered to be confused or disoriented with respect to their environment. The treatment techniques are characterized as a way of reorganizing the social structure so that the individual is encouraged and allowed to interact in a more responsible fashion.

Reality orientation attacks the aging deterioration process in two ways:

- The individual is continually stimulated through the repeated presentation of fundamental information and activities.
- The individual is placed in a relationship with the caregiver in which he or she interacts and shares with the caregiver, thereby moving from a state of withdrawal and back into the immediate environment. The relationship can help to develop a feeling of warmth and acceptance that can, in turn, generate increased participation and adaptive behavior.

Implementing a reality orientation program does not necessarily mean establishing a new program. It simply focuses attention on existing daily contacts with the individual. In any type of implementation, reality orientation is most effective when it is performed consistently on a daily basis.

The knowledge and use of various treatment models are important when you're confronted with a combination of behaviors that appear resistant to change. The underlying premise for the use of any modality is the determination that people want to improve their function and that such intervention can break the cycle of dependency and disorientation.

Reality Orientation Classes

Stages: One through Four (individuals disoriented from any cause—organic, physical, or emotional)

Location: Inside or outdoors

Equipment: Chalkboard and chalk; large calendar; large-number clock; large, colorful pictures (seasonal, animals, birds, fruits, vegetables, occupations, etc.); mirror (optional); sensory materials—for touch (e.g., fur, pinecone, pussy willow), smell (e.g., mint, aftershave, rose, eraser), hearing (e.g., ball, rhythm instruments), taste (e.g., chocolate, cracker, potato chip, banana, marshmallow), and vision (e.g., objects painted in primary colors, objects of different sizes and shapes)

Description of Activity

- Write the following headings on the chalkboard, along with the corresponding facts for each: Time, Day, Date, Month, Year, Season, Next Meal, Where We Are Living, Weather. Conduct a corresponding discussion, reinforcing what is on the board.
- Time and place:
  Review board with the following information: Address, Phone Number, Day and Time, Month, Year, Next Meal, Next Holiday.
  Practice use of calendar, clock, and time teaching aids. Teaching aids can be purchased from an educational supply store.
- Body awareness (may use mirror to look at self):
  Identify, move, and name body parts.
  Discriminate right and left.
  Draw a stick man and woman on the chalkboard and have the loved one identify which is which.

- Tactile—identifying objects by touch and responding to the sensation:

  Feel objects of different textures, such as cotton and sandpaper.

  Stimulate with objects such as paintbrushes.

- Sense of smell—identifying odors and noting similarities and differences between them:

  Present odors such as tobacco, perfume, lemon, and vanilla.

  Associate each odor with something and share the associations (e.g., "The smell of lemon reminds me of the lemon tree in the backyard").

- Hearing:

  Count how many times ball bounces.

  Listen to different rhythm instruments such as a guitar or tambourine and discuss the differences.

- Sight:

  Identify primary colors.

- Numbers: counting, writing or copying numbers, performing simple math functions such as adding and subtracting
- Money: recognizing and making change
- Sizes and shapes: identification, color recognition, comparison of sizes
- Emotions: pictures or drawings of facial expressions
- Manners: use of "Please," "Thank you," "Excuse me"

Goals: Provide mental stimulation; maintain and improve memory and socialization and restorative skills

Adaptation: These exercises for the mind can be done at any time; however, it is recommended that they be done after lunch, when most people who are living with Alzheimer's are at their peak. Early morning and evening are often times of increased confusion. You can frame the sessions as practice time, using a snack to encourage involvement. Do not get frustrated if the loved one experiences any difficulty; just focus on the positive. Keep in mind that nothing is accomplished overnight. If you are diligent and make it a fun experience, you will see some progress.

Remotivation and Reminiscing

It is universally recognized that elderly people enjoy remembering people and events from earlier years—as do most people. It is only natural that as age and disability curtail some activities and decrease feelings of productivity and usefulness, people choose to relive the periods when their sense of accomplishment was at its greatest. Reminiscence is important and beneficial to elderly people because remembering past satisfactions and successes often enables them to cope more effectively with current dissatisfactions. It is especially important to those who have Alzheimer's or dementia because their long-term memory is usually intact. They can remember things that happened twenty years ago but may have difficulty remembering what they had for breakfast that morning. Demonstrating the ability to remember enhances their self-esteem.

Caregivers should encourage the positive reminiscences of elderly people. The use of reminiscence can help to establish rapport and increase participation in activities. The caregiver should actively seek projects that stimulate involvement. Families have an excellent opportunity to contribute because they usually have family pictures and other mementos readily available.

Remotivation therapy is a simple technique in which elderly people are encouraged to remember the happy and rewarding experiences of earlier years. The caregiver should stimulate reminiscences by using various aids such as poems, pictures, or stories. Those who have employed this technique have reported many positive results.

Remotivation

In most disorders of elderly people involving confusion and withdrawal, parts of the person's original personality remain relatively untouched. Frequently, the healthy, "untouched" parts have to do with everyday, ordinary things that many of us take for granted, such as what items are sold in a department store or the way a tree grows. Remotivation is a form of group-based therapy built on five essential steps. Its purpose is to encourage moderately confused people to become more interested in their surroundings by focusing their attention on simple, objective topics that are not related to their limitations.

Although originally designed as a technique for use with people suffering from mental illness, remotivation has been found to be applicable in many other cases, including among people who have physical disorders, people who are confused, and people who are recovering from strokes. The activities focus on helping withdrawn but alert persons to regain the motivation and self-confidence needed to engage in larger social activities.

Sessions should last from twenty to thirty minutes and be conducted consistently each week. Each session is organized around an objective topic of conversation, which is discussed through five steps: Climate of Acceptance, Bridge to the Real World, Sharing the World We Live In, Appreciation of the Work of the World, and Climate of Appreciation. Objects, pictures, music, and/or poetry may be used to meet individual needs.

Ideas

- Caregivers should ask family members to provide photographs of the loved one and his or her parents from earlier years to be displayed attractively and predominately around the home. These may be used repeatedly at various holidays such as Mother's Day and Father's Day. Also ask for photographs of the person's hometown or country of origin from a specific period or prior to a specific year, and display them in open view. Photographs from their hometown or country can stimulate memories from childhood and early adulthood. Sometimes certain historical events took place during the person's growing-up period, such as World War I and II. Years such as the year their children were born or the years they graduated or got married have special meaning and therefore can stimulate thoughts and discussions. According to research done by Stanford University, the years when someone was between the ages of twenty and forty have the strongest effect upon stimulating memories.

- Display photos of the loved one at younger ages, with young children, with friends, and so forth. On holidays, display any photos you may have of earlier family celebrations of the holiday.

- Decorate the loved one's room with family pictures and mementos from the past. Encourage the person to keep photo albums in the room.

- Use a tape recorder to encourage the person to record as many memories as possible about one significant event in his or her life, such as a great flood, a heavy snowfall, World War II, or Prohibition. Although this activity is geared toward people in Stages One and Two, the long-term memory may still be intact with Stage Three and oftentimes Stage Four people. Assist with operating the machine as needed. Stages Three and Four may also have difficulty forming thoughts or speaking; monitor for this and discontinue activity if it is too hard for them. To prompt the discussion, you may also say, for example, "I heard that during World War II sugar was severely rationed out." They may just nod their head in acknowledgment as to yes or no, and although this type of interaction may not be helpful in recording, it may stimulate loved ones to actually verbalize their thoughts.

- Play recordings of popular songs from earlier eras, and arrange sing-alongs of old songs. (See the Music chapter for more ideas.)

- Play charades and act out activities of the past, such as washing on a scrub board or driving a buggy.

Reminiscing Kits

Stages: One through Four

Location: Inside, in-room, or outdoors

Equipment: Varies with kit

Description of Activity

▪ Prepare one or more of the following kits. Each kit should contain ten to twenty items to be viewed, handled, and discussed. Make sure nothing is included that could cause injury. For example, the shaving kit should contain a razor without a blade; the tackle box should have lures with no hooks.

Woman's purse containing items such as an eyeglass case with
*   sunglasses, a compact with mirror, brush and comb, billfold with*
*   pictures, gloves, perfume, hand lotion, and keys*
Man's shaving kit
Diaper bag
Fishing tackle box
Gardening kit
Laundry basket with items to be folded, a miniature ironing
*   board, an iron with the cord cut off, a sprinkling bottle, and so*
*   forth*
Kitchen kit
School kit

Goals: Maintain and improve memory and object recognition

Family History Scrapbook

Stages: One and Two; Stage Three with assistance

Location: Inside

Equipment: Paper and pencils

Description of Activity

- Prepare several sheets of paper with various questions pertaining to your loved one's history. (See accompanying examples.)
- Work together at a table. Supply pencils, and tell the person to use his or her imagination, memory, and writing skills to answer the questions on the page. Stress that there are no wrong answers, only the sharing of information. It should be an open discussion.
- When the loved one is finished, invite him or her to read the answers aloud if you think the person would be comfortable doing so. Encourage discussion of the answers.
- Be prepared to stimulate discussion; however, this will probably not be necessary, as the loved one will likely take over the discussion.
- Each session should run about one hour. Schedule this activity once or twice monthly. After each session, compile the loved one's papers in a scrapbook. You can present a new set of questions each time and reinforce periodically, as needed.
- Invite the whole family to join in the fun!
- If your loved one cannot write, try using a tape recorder, and then transcribe the responses at a later time. Your loved one could also dictate answers for you to write down.

Goals: Have fun!; increase self-esteem through reliving fond memories; maintain and improve hand-eye coordination and small motor skills (Precaution: Watch for emotional reactions; this is not necessarily bad.)

A Few of My Favorite Things

My favorite color is _____

My favorite food is _____

My favorite president is, or was _____

My favorite song is _____

My favorite famous person is _____

My favorite year was _____

My reasons for choosing that year are _____

_____

_____

_____

_____

About Me

My name is _____

I was born in the year _____ in _____ (city/state/country)

I was married in the year _____ in _____ (city/state/country)

My first child was born _____

I would describe myself as _____

_____

_____

_____

_____

_____

_____

_____

_____

_____

_____

Day _____

Date _____

Year _____

Signature _____

Places I Have Been

Vacations _____

My favorite vacation was _____

. . . because _____

_____

_____

When I was in the military I went to _____

_____

I have lived in _____

_____

My favorite place to live was _____

. . . because _____

My Youth

Mother _____

Father _____

Brothers and sisters _____

_____

My favorite relative is _____

. . . because _____

My fondest memory is _____

_____

_____

_____

My favorite middle school memory is _____

_____

_____

My favorite high school memory is _____

_____

_____

My happiest memory after high school is _____

_____

_____

_____

Guess It/Match It Discussion Time

Stages: One and Two

Location: Inside

Equipment: Three-by-five-inch note cards or pieces of paper; pen or pencil

Description of Activity

▪ Provide each person with enough paper for each question to be asked, usually about fifteen to twenty, and a pen or pencil.

▪ Explain that you are going to ask a question, and the person should write down the first thing that comes to mind. There are no incorrect answers, and answers should not be spoken aloud.

▪ Ask the first question. If you are doing this with only the loved one, after the person has written the answer, ask him or her to show it to you, and then discuss it. If you have several participants, have them show their answers one at a time, and see how many of them came up with the same answer.

▪ Sample questions might be, "What is the hottest month of the year? The coldest?"; "When does it rain the most?"; "What does a red light mean? Yellow light? Green light?"; "What kind of cat or dog do you think is cute?"; "What is the sweetest fruit?"; "What is the best food for breakfast?"

▪ Continue with remaining questions. The game is over after all questions are discussed or at the end of an allotted time period, usually thirty to forty-five minutes.

Goals: Strengthen small motor skills, hand-eye coordination, memory recall, and self-esteem; encourage mental imaging

Reminiscence Time

This activity is great anytime. It promotes good times, shared laughter, and smiles. It can be really helpful to do in the evening prior to bedtime. Often going to sleep with good memories and a smile on your face helps one sleep through the night. It also makes a great distraction activity. Often when someone is frustrated with current problems, it helps to be able to think of good memories, and with Alzheimer's, long-term memory is usually intact.

Description of Activity

■ Topical discussion: Choose one topic with which the loved one and any other participants may relate and that may generate positive memories—for example, "summer fun." Provide a poem and paraphernalia related to the topic to stimulate memories. For the "summer fun" example, these props could include baseball cards, peanuts, photos of strawberry hullers, a handheld fan, and a nose clip used in swimming. Have participants look through advertisements in the day's newspaper and compare the prices of items related to the topic with what prices were in the past. Everyone gets a laugh at the change. This activity is perfect for after dinner, as it provides a nice calming transition before bedtime and can send everyone off with a smile.

■ Reminiscence journalism group: Set aside a series of times during which the loved one writes remembrances of past days. The remembrances should proceed chronologically, from early childhood through adult years. Families love sharing the memories—typed and photocopied for posterity. The collection makes an excellent gift for the whole family. Photos can be added for that extra touch.

■ Toys and games: Engage the loved one in traditional activities such as dominoes, building blocks, puzzles, memory games, and so forth. A variety of memory games are availabe as educational toys.

▪ Reading *National Geographic*: Seat the loved one close to you, and read from issues of *National Geographic*, pointing out compelling pictures as you read to stimulate talk about foreign countries.

▪ Educational movies: Have a weekly movie hour. Many libraries have good collections of films on video featuring topics such as art, anthropology, biography, history, and music. These are excellent for mental stimulation and great for reminiscing.

▪ Musical expressions: In the evening, listen to a variety of music on the radio or TV music channels. Various forms, from Broadway reviews to classic radio shows, are available. Afterward, encourage the loved one to discuss and reminisce. It's a good way to relax before bedtime.

▪ Brainteasers: Play Trivial Pursuit; play along with television game shows such as "Family Feud" and "The Price Is Right"; work crossword puzzles; play hangman; have spelling bees.

▪ Current events: Attach magazine pictures of people in the news to a bulletin board or poster board under a heading such as "Guess My Name" or "Who Am I?" Clip newspaper articles about happenings in your city or neighborhood, as well as local and national news, and discuss them.

Restorative Activities

The activities in this chapter are designed to improve or maintain your loved one's ability to perform the activities of daily living, such as eating, dressing, and preparing simple foods. The focus is on being independent for as long as possible and restoring lost skills. There does not have to be a specific time set aside for these activities; merely incorporate them into your daily routine.

Many adaptations can be made with respect to eating utensils and aids in dressing, such as a scoop dish with a nonskid bottom to avoid shoving food off the table or handles with rubber grips for easier handling. Many simple aids that help with dressing are now available. There are items to assist with buttons, pulling on clothing, arranging blankets while in bed, and picking up items. If your loved one is having difficulty with any aspect of his or her care, it is a good idea to request an occupational therapy consult from your physician. A physician can evaluate your loved one and suggest appropriate adaptive equipment.

A Word About Behavior

Often persons living with Alzheimer's disease will act inappropriately on many occasions and in different settings. This includes a range of possibilities such as washing their dentures in a cup of coffee in a restaurant, reacting to fear in a shower, and removing their clothing in public. People with Alzheimer's or any other kind of dementia oftentimes do strange things simply because their cognitive abilities have been affected by the disease process. Nearly all social behavior is learned and therefore it can be unlearned or forgotten during the process of the disease. This may also lead to emotional outbreaks of anger, frustration, denial, and even catastrophic reactions. Catastrophic reactions are when they overreact to an event or stimulus, in the form of anger, fear, anxiety, grief, or any other powerful emotion. The best way to cope with any behavior demonstrated by your loved one is to show humor, kindness, and understanding. Below are a few tips to help the caregiver handle situations:

- Do not ask a person with Alzheimer's why he or she did something odd. Instead, indicate in a nonjudgmental manner what you would like the person to do; for example, say, "It is probably not a good idea to wash your dentures in the coffee. Perhaps you can put them back in your mouth and we can wash them when we get home. OK?"
- Avoid becoming angry or frustrated; this only makes things worse. If you become agitated, so will the person you are caring for.
- Never confront; only persuade.
- Never give orders—make suggestions.

- Give plenty of time for preparations.
- Allow plenty of time for the loved one to assimilate what is being said.
- Gently explain what is going on in a simple way.
- Do not try to force any situation.
- Use your imagination compassionately.
- Do not try to prove them wrong through logical rationale: they know their feelings and will not be argued out of them.
- Use distraction by initiating a new activity.
- Remove them from the source of the agitation. Remember, most episodes of behavior problems are reactive.
- Use a car ride to soothe distressed feelings.
- Ignore the anger; leave them alone a few minutes to vent their frustrations if at home. Let them know you will return in a few minutes.
- Remember, behavior often becomes worse or exaggerated late at night, so plan around this.
- Always listen and offer emotional support.
- Look for underlying reasons for any type of agitation. Some of the most common are listed here:
  - *exhaustion*
  - *boredom*
  - *emotional stress*
  - *loneliness*
  - *grief*
  - *fear*
  - *feeling useless*
  - *pain*
  - *illness*

- Add a nap during the day.
- Offer energy snacks.
- Offer unconditional acceptance.
- Understand the reality of the situation and the nature of the problem before making a decision.
- Look for workable solutions. For example, if the one you are caring for keeps taking off his or her clothing late in the evening, it might be better to just shut the curtains. It may not always be the solution you want, but it is the best workable solution.

The Community Outings chapter has more information about behavior in social situations.

Kitchen Orientation

Stages: One through Three

Location: Kitchen

Equipment: Standard kitchen items, as described

Description of Activity

- Have the loved one wash and dry hands prior to eating and preparing food.
- Ask the loved one to name and identify basic kitchen utensils, such as a can opener, bottle opener, vegetable peeler, grater, strainer, and spatula. The caregiver can name an object and have the loved one point to it, or the caregiver can point to an object and have the loved one name it. It also works very well during

any meal preparation; for example, ask, "Can you show me the whisk?" while whipping eggs.

■ Ask the person to explain the function of each of the utensils named.

■ Ask the person to identify the parts of a stove, including burners, temperature control, and oven.

■ For Stages One and Two, ask the person to boil enough water for a cup of tea or a hard-boiled egg. You may need to cue the person as far as what container to use and how much water is needed. Be sure to supervise throughout.

■ Ask the person to distinguish between foods that have to be cooked and those that can be eaten raw, such as apples, meat, celery, macaroni, lettuce, chicken, fish, eggs.

■ For Stages One and Two, ask the person to use a knife to cut a sandwich in half or slice a banana. Be sure to supervise throughout.

■ For Stages One and Two, supervise as the person prepares a simple meal using some of the items previously identified—such as soup and a sandwich. Although at these stages most people can still recognize and have the desire to consume meals, it may still be necessary for the caregiver to suggest the time and an appropriate meal. If slicing is necessary, supervise the person for proper use and safety procedures with a knife. The caregiver should cue as needed and supervise the use of the stove or microwave.

■ Ask the person to properly set the table.

■ Ask the person to measure different types of food, such as dry goods (rice, flour, sugar) and liquids (water, milk, oil) in the following amounts: one-fourth cup, one-half cup, and one cup.

■ Ask the loved one to tell you the different ways to cook certain foods, such as meats: roast, bake, fry, broil. Answers will vary according to the food choices. For example, eggs have many answers: boiled, poached, hard-boiled, fried (soft, over medium, sunny side up, hard), scrambled, just to name a few. Cue the person as needed; sometimes you may also need to help with the answers.

Goals: Maintain and improve ability to function independently in the area of food preparation, as well as memory and object recognition

Self-Help: Preparation and Consumption of Simple Foods

Stages: One and Two

Location: Kitchen

Equipment: Standard kitchen items, as described

Description of Activity

▪ Have the loved one wash and dry hands prior to eating and preparing food.

▪ Ask the person to identify the following eating utensils: fork, spoon, knife, glass, plate.

▪ Monitor for the proper use of fork, knife, spoon, and napkin.

▪ Ask the loved one to demonstrate drinking from a cup, glass, straw, and can.

▪ Ask the loved one to pour liquid into a glass from a pitcher or large container, open a bottle with a twist-off cap and a can with a snap-off lid.

▪ Ask the person to wash and peel simple foods, such as apples.

- Ask the person to spread butter or jelly on bread.
- Supervise for appropriate table manners.

Goals: Maintain and increase independence in the area of preparation and consumption of simple foods, as well as memory and object recognition skills

Dressing and Care of Clothes

Stages: One through Three

Location: Inside, in-room

Equipment: Items of clothing as described

Description of Activity

- Ask the loved one to identify the following items: hat, belt, shirt, coat, pants, jacket, nightclothes.
- Ask the person to demonstrate the proper skills with buttons, zippers, snaps, and buckles.
- Ask the person to properly match an outfit.
- Hold up pictures of different seasons and activities—golf, swimming, rain, autumn leaves—and ask what the appropriate clothing would be for that situation.

Goals: Maintain and increase independence in the area of dressing, as well as memory and object recognition skills

Sensory Stimulation

Sensory stimulation consists of activities and procedures involving the kinesthetic, tactile, olfactory, auditory, visual, and gustatory senses that orient people to their environment. Regressed elderly people show an inability to interact with the environment due to physical and memory problems. This condition is complicated by rejection and withdrawal. The goal of sensory stimulation is to increase sensitivity to stimuli and awareness of the environment through stimulation of all sensory receptors. Emphasis is placed on individual stimulation.

Bed-bound persons are at a much higher risk for self-isolation and decreased cognitive functioning due to the decreased opportunities for everyday sensory stimulation. However, it is equally important that non–bed-bound persons receive adequate sensory stimulation. Even though they may have more opportunities to be stimulated throughout the day by everyday sounds and smells, it is important to stimulate all senses to prevent further loss of memory.

Individual Sensory Stimulation

- Sessions are held at the bedside of bed-bound persons and any comfortable setting for non-bed-bound persons, and last for approximately three to ten minutes.
- Music, songs, and sounds provide stimulation to the auditory sense and are accompanied by verbal cues and suggestions. Brightly colored objects and pictures stimulate sight. Objects of various textures and, especially, the use of human touch stimulate the tactile sense. Various odors and fragrances stimulate the olfactory sense. The gustatory sense is stimulated by familiar foods and flavors. Exercises, which stress direction ability (the ability to retain and follow written or verbal instructions) and movement of the body in space, stimulate the kinesthetic sense.
- Progress is measured by increases in basic behaviors such as eye contact, appropriate body movements, and attention span.

Environmental Awareness

- Individual sensory stimulation is given in a quiet setting for people who are nonverbal, low functioning, or in Stage Four. For those in Stages One through Three, any comfortable setting will work well.

- In addition to the sensory stimulation activities, multi-sensory music activities are used to stimulate eye contact, active participation in instrumental and movement activities, awareness of others and the environment, and appropriate verbalizations. Emphasis is placed on body awareness.
- Again, progress is measured by increases in eye contact, purposeful manipulation of objects, and appropriate verbalizations, and changes in affect or display of emotions.

Sensory Stimulation Ideas

Stages: One through Four

Location: Inside or outdoors

Equipment: Theme-specific decorations or props; theme colors

Suggestions for Various Senses
- Olfactory—baking bread, holiday smells, milk, lemonade, yeast in water, chocolate, Limburger cheese, oranges
- Auditory—poems, song lyrics, short stories, holiday songs, rhythm instruments such as bells
- Tactile—rolling pin, grass, old milk bottle, dough, milk carton, felt
- Visual—loaf of bread, holiday picture, pictures of cows, city pictures, videotapes, old movies

▪ Taste—bread and butter, milk, shaved chocolate, chopped hard-boiled egg, sweet and sour tastes

▪ Magazines are good sources for pictures and readings.

Description of Activity

▪ Pick a theme, such as what you'd find at the grocery store, a picnic, or certain holiday, prior to the activity and arrange supporting props.

▪ Explore all the ideas associated with the theme. For example, for a Christmas theme, speak of past Christmas experiences, bring in the Christmas colors (red, white, green), sounds of bells, pictures of Santa Claus, talk about individual beliefs associated with Christmas, foods associated with the Christmas dinner, and poinsettia plants, etc.

▪ Start by singing a song. "He's Got the Whole World in His Hands" is a tried-and-true example. Invite your loved one to sing, clap, or participate in any other way desired. Then shake hands, hug, or caress.

▪ Continue by using props from the list. If time allows, play a song, preferably with an upbeat tempo, and invite the loved one to accompany on a rhythm instrument. Bells are the best because they come equipped with handles.

▪ Close by singing an appropriate favorite song ("So Long, It's Been Good to Know You" works well if you're parting company).

Goals: Stimulate all five senses

Flower Petal Massage

Stages: One through Four

Location: Inside or outdoors

Equipment: Flowers

Description of Activity

■ When flower arrangements begin to wilt, have your loved one remove the flower petals and place them on a tray or in a flat basket.

■ Ask the person to tell you what kind of flower the petals are from. Suggest that the loved one place his or her hands on the petals. For nonverbal loved ones, ask questions such as, "Do they feel soft?"—yes or no questions—and watch for nonverbal reactions, such as a head nod, eye contact, or a smile.

■ You can shower the petals over the person's hands or rub hands softly with the petals.

Goals: Provide new sensory experiences—tactile and visual; provide opportunity for sharing past experiences—an event when the person received flowers, for example

Adaptation: Other uses for discarded flowers include pressing them and making potpourri or sachets (see Arts and Crafts chapter).

Bundles of Smells

Stages: One through Four

Location: Inside or outdoors

Equipment: Cheesecloth; scissors; variety of fragrant herbs and spices, such as cinnamon, cloves, cumin, nutmeg, and basil; pieces of fruit; small rubber bands

Description of Activity

■ Cut the cheesecloth into small squares—one for each ingredient. Put a few teaspoons of one herb, spice, or fruit in the center of a square, gather the cloth together at the top, and secure it with a rubber band. Continue making individual "bundles of smells."

■ Ask your loved one to sniff each bundle individually. (Some people, especially those in Stage Four, may try to eat the bundles, so this activity usually requires one-on-one attention.)

■ Being able to identify the scent is not important. Do not press for the correct name, but rather ask if the scent is pleasant, what it smells like, or if it evokes a memory of something—for example, cinnamon reminds some people of toast.

■ Use the exercise as an opportunity to initiate discussions about memories, cooking, and other topics.

Goals: Determine extent of ability to smell; stimulate any intact ability; encourage verbalization, description, and socialization; stimulate memories, possibly leading to discussion; encourage bonding between the caregiver and loved one

Touch Grab Bag

Stages: One through Four

Location: Inside, in-room, or outdoors

Equipment: Items of different textures, such as cotton balls, sandpaper, and rocks; pillowcase

Description of Activity

- Gather items of different textures and place them in the pillowcase.
- Tell your loved one to reach into the pillowcase and pick up one item without looking at it.
- Then ask him or her to identify the item based on its texture and shape. Give verbal clues if needed such as, "Is it soft?" or "Is it round?"
- If the loved one is hesitant to reach into the bag without seeing the contents first, let him or her look in the bag to reduce fear.
- Continue until all of the items have been labeled.

Goals: Utilize and strengthen memory recall; provide tactile stimulation; encourage discussion; provide a challenge

Adaptation: For low-functioning people in Stages Three and Four, place only one or two items in the bag at one time. You can also put common functional objects in the bag, such as a toothbrush, a hairbrush, or a handkerchief; when the item is selected, assist the person in using it.

Play-Doh Power

Stages: One through Four

Location: Inside, in-room, or outdoors

Equipment: Various colors of Play-Doh; cookie cutters and rolling pins

Description of Activity

- Provide adequate workspace.
- Allow the person to choose which of the colors of Play-Doh to use.
- Explain how to roll, hit, press, and squeeze the material to form it into any shape desired.
- Make cookie cutters and rolling pins available as well, but do not associate this activity with making cookies, which could cause some people to sample the imaginary cookies!
- Monitor to avoid possible attempts to eat the Play-Doh. (However, Play-Doh is used instead of clay because it is nontoxic and will not be harmful if swallowed.)
- Allow this activity to be unstructured and casual. Do not push for participation.

Goals: Provide tactile stimulation and outlet for nervous energy or anxiety; strengthen small motor control, hand-eye coordination, and self-esteem

Adaptation: Use the occasion to involve smaller children in the household.

Socialization Activities

As Alzheimer's progresses, people afflicted tend to self-isolate. This is a protective measure against the outside world, deriving from their knowledge of their limitations. However, if the isolation continues, it will have a detrimental effect on their self-esteem, well-being, and health.

Often, when people are encouraged to begin socialization again, it is easier and more comfortable for them to interact with their same sex. Take things slowly; start with family and close friends, and then gradually enlarge the social interactions.

Ladies' Luncheon

Stages: One through Four

Locations: Inside or outdoors

Equipment: Tablecloths; fresh flowers; music; decorations; invitations

Description of Activity

- Carefully choose a menu—something elegant and different.
- Make it something special according to the person's likes and dislikes. Keep in mind that persons should be invited according to whom the loved one is comfortable with.
- The food can either be brought in from a favorite restaurant or cooked by the family. It should be something that is special and well-liked by your loved one. It is always nice to have someone serve the meal—this can be the caregiver, a family member, or someone from an outside catering service. The purpose is to make the affair resemble a restaurant outing as much as possible.

Goals: Provide a restaurant-type meal and a chance to socialize for ladies who, by choice or physical disability, are unable to go out to eat; increase socialization skills and trust and bonding between the caregiver and loved one

Men's Workshop

Stages: One and Two

Locations: Outdoors or in a workroom

Equipment: Vises, C-clamps, or tape; tools such as hammers, nails, and leatherwork implements; construction materials such as lumber scraps, copper sheeting, and jute; wood glue and leather glue; shoe polish—paste and liquid, to be used as stain; polyurethane sealer (Check labels on all chemicals for flammability and proper storing procedure.)

Description of Activity

■ Use vises, C-clamps, or tape as necessary to secure items to the worktable.

■ Project ideas include plaques, macramé plant hangers and wall hangings, napkin holders, picture frames, bird feeders, and copper tooling pictures.

■ Use your creativity when working with the loved one. The average project should take no more than three sessions to complete, with a work period of one hour per session. Many activities of this nature can be found at arts and crafts stores, hobbie shops, or your local home improvement center. Make sure that each activity notes the time span needed to complete the project.

Goals: Create a masculine atmosphere; increase self-confidence; maintain and improve hand–eye coordination, object recognition, and ability to follow two-step and three-step directions

Facials—for Women

Stages: One through Four

Locations: Inside

Equipment: Lounge chair; makeup remover; warm face towels; paper towels; cotton balls; hydrating facial mask; facial cream; facial toner; assorted makeup; perfume; coffee or other refreshments

Description of Activity
- Invite women from among friends and family.
- Arrange all equipment on a large table.
- Seat participants in the lounge chair, each taking a turn.
- Remove makeup with hypoallergenic makeup remover and a cotton ball. Use warm towels to assist on any facial cleaning.
- Apply hydrating facial mask according to manufacturer's instructions.
- Remove mask and cleanse face with facial cream.
- Apply a bit more of the facial cream after the mask has been removed and massage face with gentle upward strokes for two or three minutes. Avoid rubbing around the eyes because the skin can be very delicate in this area.
- Wipe off excess cream with cotton ball and apply facial toner.
- Makeup can now be applied (see Grooming chapter).
- Serve refreshments.

Goals: Promote self-esteem and self-care; increase socialization skills; create a nice relaxing atmosphere to promote bonding between the caregiver and loved one.

Note: do not re-use items on different persons without first disinfecting, cleaning, or soaking the items. You can use rubbing alcohol to disinfect. This will prevent spreading germs among the persons using the equipment.

Poker Night

There are countless poker variations around the world, but many of them, such as draw and stud, are universal. Poker has traditionally been associated with men's night out and, as such, will make a nice addition to any plans to get the "guys" together.

Stages: One and Two; Three with assistance

Locations: Inside or outside

Equipment: One deck of playing cards; gambling chips; table large enough to sit six; refreshments, such as cheese and crackers, chips and dip, sausages, alcoholic and soft drinks as appropriate, popcorn, pretzels, shelled peanuts

Description of Activity
- Invite four to six men over to play. Allot ample time (at least two hours) for the loved one and his male companions to enjoy each other's company.
- Set table up with ample supply of snack foods and refreshments.
- Establish betting rules and know the lingo:
  Bet: number of chips that can be wagered, or put in the pot.
  Call: a player matches the amount bet.

Check or pass: If no bets have been made, a player may wish to pass the turn to the left.

Fold: If unwilling to call a bet or raise, the player drops out of the hand losing his initial bet.

Raise: Set amount that a player can raise the bet, over and above the original bet. (Other players must meet this amount.)

Re-raises: Usually limited to three raises per hand.

- Establish rules of etiquette before playing:

Plays should be made in turn.

A bet announced is a bet made.

Hands should not be discussed.

Players must guard their hand.

Bets cannot be changed until the re-raise.

- Play the game:

Once a dealer has been chosen, usually by a cut of the deck (the one who gets the largest valued amount of card is the dealer), the deal is passed to the left.

Everyone antes up the beginning bet.

Players are dealt five cards facedown; they may discard any number of cards and redraw the same amount of cards.

The draw is followed by raising, folding, or re-raising.

The winning hand gets the pot.

Goals: Make men feel special; improve or maintain memory and directional ability skills; provide avenue for socialization; promote bonding

Adaptation: This activity can be designed to fit any favorite game, such as dominoes, chess, backgammon, or checkers. It can also be adapted for women by playing their games of choice.

Super Bowl Party

Super Bowl parties always inspire memories of great times. The excitement of watching the best athletes compete is very stimulating. Other sports can be substituted for football as well. Men can bond and share memories from other games. It is just great fun all around.

Stages: One through Four

Locations: Inside

Equipment: Television; tapes of previous Super Bowl games; refreshments such as chips and dip, hot dogs, cheese and crackers, pretzels, popcorn or any type of snack foods; alcohol and soft drinks as appropriate; decorations according to the football theme

Description of Activity

■ Allow for ample uninterrupted time to view the game. This can be either a current Super Bowl or taped Super Bowl games from the past. This way the Super Bowl can happen more than once a year.

■ Arrange for comfortable sitting arrangements for all who are participating.

■ Provide plenty of snack foods and refreshments.

■ Encourage fun and laughs.

Goals: To make men feel special, since they are usually a minority in a population surrounded by and cared for mostly by women; increase social skills; promote bonding between caregiver and loved one

Adaptation: This can be adapted to any game, such as golf, tennis, or basketball. The goal is to get the "guys" together and have male bonding time.

Breakfast Club

Everyone likes receiving invitations. It turns an everyday occurrence into a special event. So, when you form breakfast club, it is a nice idea to distribute invitations. Invitations of your choice can be sent to family members, friends, or others who are living with Alzheimer's.

Prior to the first meeting in your home, it is a good idea to obtain the likes, dislikes, and any special diet restrictions from all persons who will be attending. This will assist you in planning a menu. If more than six people will be attending, a buffet style menu usually works the best.

Stages: One and Two

Locations: Participants' choice

Equipment: Invitations; if the group will meet in your home, you'll need tableware, food, and other supplies

Description of Activity
- Distribute invitations to form a breakfast group.
- Select a specific time and day of the month and a location—for example, the third Wednesday of the month, 7:30 A.M., Sky Lounge.
- Send invitations to each participant for the initial group meeting.

■ If the meeting is at your home, set the table and prepare the food.

■ Serve the food family style to increase sensory awareness.

■ Facilitate conversation by introducing people to each other and raising topics for conversation.

■ Thank each participant for coming and state the time and place for the next session.

Goals: Provide a nonthreatening, pleasant activity to promote social interaction for people living with Alzheimer's; involve people who hesitate to engage in other activities in a social dining experience

Adaptation: This can be done in conjunction with other Alzheimer's groups in the community. Contact your local Alzheimer's association for times and dates of meetings of support groups. This activity could also be adapted for lunch or dinner clubs.

More Activity Ideas

One-on-One and In-Room Visits

There may well be times when the person who is being cared for is bed-bound. The condition may be either temporary or chronic and long-term. Activities are especially important for people who are in this type of forced isolation. A specific amount of time—usually a minimum of one hour per day—should be set aside for these one-on-one activities; however, they may also take place spontaneously. The person may even already have an activity schedule.

Activity includes all of the interactions in which an individual is engaged, not necessarily a specific program. Try to promote activities that can be done alone without supervision. For example, an alert bed-bound person may be interested in writing letters, thank-you notes, or articles for the family newsletter; doing artwork; making items for bazaars; or engaging in similar hobbies that keep the individual an integral part of the community.

People with Alzheimer's and dementia hold great concern to us because they are isolated as a result of the debilitating disease and its associated confusion and depression. Their motivation is at its lowest, and it is difficult and often impossible to find out about their previous lifestyle patterns and interests. They require time! The suggestions that follow should help.

Motivational Cart

A traveling "motivational cart" containing a variety of items often will spark or cultivate an interest or provide a focal point for conversation. A rolling garden cart found at most garden shops or a rolling serving tray found at any department store makes an excellent motivational cart. Don't limit yourself! Look around and see what is available. Just about any activity can be adapted for use in single rooms. For example, the avid fly fisher might enjoy fly tying, looking at pictures of favorite fishing spots, or swapping fish stories with someone.

Here are some possibilities for stocking your traveling motivational cart for use when providing an activity for a person who is confined to a bed or a room:

- Record, cassette, or CD player with a variety of recordings, including music and Books on Tape, as well as tapes of old radio shows—often available through the local library
- Playing cards—regular and large-print
- Games for one, such as electronic games, and for two, such as Scrabble and checkers
- Craft projects—small and simple but adult oriented

- Sketching materials, including tablets, pencils, and art erasers
- Writing materials, including stationery, everyday cards, pens, and stamps
- Books—regular and large-print—in a variety of genres, such as western, mystery, biography, poetry, spiritual, history, and comedy
- Current newspapers—metropolitan and/or local
- TV schedules—with programs of interest identified by either the caregiver or loved one
- Current magazines
- Regular and large-print crossword puzzles and other word games
- Textured items—to feel and identify in a simple game with you or someone else—such as sandpaper, wood, velvet, cotton, and sponge
- Variously shaped items—also for use in a game—such as clothespin, key, triangle, ball, bell, and stuffed animal
- Treats, such as fresh fruit, candy, and popcorn; food often promotes conversation
- One or two fresh flowers
- Jigsaw puzzles—small and regular size
- Project boards: these are twenty-four-inch squares of fiberboard, with half-inch molding on all sides to prevent things from slipping off; the board can serve as a handy base for jigsaw puzzle enthusiasts and others and can be slid under the bed when not in use
- Decorations appropriate to the current holiday or season, tray favors, and the like
- Notions, such as needles, thread, thimbles, scissors, crocheting items, and knitting materials

Sensation Time: Sensory-Stimulating Activities

- Have a different theme weekly—for example, Sweet and Sour Day, Smooth and Rough Day, Loud and Quiet Day—and use appropriate items to convey it. Put the items in a bag and have the person feel inside the bag and try to figure out what each item is.
- The same idea can be applied to smells: place various fragrances on cotton balls and ask what each smells like. You can also use different flavors for taste and different materials for touch. Ask the person to tell you about the fragrance, taste, or texture.

Master List of In-Room Activities

- Acrylic painting
- Ant farm
- Balloon messages (have a nice day, happy birthday, etc.)
- Balloon volleyball
- Books on Tape
- Ceramics
- Checkers
- Clay
- Collages from magazines
- Crocheting
- Crossword puzzles
- Discussion of current events
- Drawing
- Etching
- Exercises
- Fishbowl
- Flower arranging
- Lap quilting
- Letter writing
- Life history journals
- Listening to tapes
- Manicure
- Mending
- Musical keyboard
- Mobile making
- Needlepointing
- Ornaments
- Pen pals
- Pets
- Poetry
- Puzzles
- Radio
- Reading
- Records

- Reminiscing
- Scrapbooks
- Solitaire
- Stained glass
- Stenciling
- Table games
- Telephone

- Terrarium
- Tutoring
- TV
- Typing on a laptop
- Writing fiction or nonficiton

Enjoying Pets and Other Animals

Just like sunshine and a good diet, pets or interaction with animals is just plain healthy for the elderly. They are a sparkplug for interaction and increased socialization, and they bring a smile to the face. Animals provide an avenue for nonjudgmental warmth and affection. Pets encourage playfulness, laughter, and increased exercise. Research has proven that interacting with or owning a pet provides the following benefits. Seniors who interact with pets on a regular basis:

- Go to the doctor less often
- Have lower tryglycerides and cholesterol levels
- Have a higher level of social interaction and verbal interaction
- Have decreased feelings of loneliness and isolation
- Demonstrate a higher level of optimism
- Satisfy their need for touch and to be touched
- Exhibit a decreased deterioration rate in ADLs
- Demonstrate less fear in new situations
- Have decreased depression
- Show decreased episodes of hypertension

Ideas

- Have a "Farm Day" outdoors: arrange for small farm animals to be brought in for a visit by 4-H or FFA students, perhaps in conjunction with a picnic.
- Contact the local humane society or animal shelter to arrange to participate in a visiting animal program; ask for an obedience demonstration.
- Contact local zoos to arrange for visits from traveling zoos.
- Ask a 4-H group or dog or cat fancier group to come and present a mini pet show.
- Have your own mini pet show with pets in the household. Ask family members, friends, and others to bring in their pets and join the fun.
- Learn more about pet therapy through the website http://pettherapy.meetup.com. Although pet therapy meet-ups is available online only, they are the very best in providing contacts.
- Place a fish tank with large, brightly colored fish in the room or elsewhere in the residence. Even a confused person can watch and enjoy the fish, which have interest value and provide stimulus.
- Place wild bird feeders outside the windows. Post a chart picturing the birds likely to visit the feeders on a nearby wall to aid in identification.

Goals

The goals associated with pet-visiting activities are varied and include the following: help to alleviate effects of chronic disability or illness, depression, sense of loss regarding a previous relationship with pets, loneliness and isolation, feelings of helplessness, low self-esteem, hopelessness, and absence of humor; provide the unbounded love and unqualified approval that pets can give; lead the person and family members to new interests; provide an opportunity for verbalization, sensory stimulation, and reminiscing.

Special Considerations

Prior to the activity, address the following issues with the one providing the animals:

- Make sure that any animal that comes into contact with people or other animals is clean and healthy, has all required immunizations, and is temperamentally suitable and predictable—friendly, calm, and under control. A veterinarian's involvement here is essential.
- Visiting animals should be on a leash or in an appropriate cage.
- Animals should be exercised before the visit, and materials should be available for promptly cleaning up any accidents and disinfecting the area.
- Animals should be kept out of food preparation and serving areas.
- Assure that anyone who wants to avoid animals because of allergy, fear, or any other reason does not have to come in contact with them.

Should a scratch or injury occur to a person, obtain all information regarding shot record, veterinarian, and contact information from the one providing the animal.

Bibliography

Aronson, M., ed. *Understanding Alzheimer's Disease: What It Is, How to Cope with It, Future Directions.* New York: Scribner's, 1988.

Barg, G. *The Fearless Caregiver: How to Get the Best for Your Loved One and Still Have a Life of Your Own.* Hendon, VA: Capital Books, 2001.

Bell, V., and D. Troxel. *A Dignified Life: The Best Friend's Approach to Alzheimer's Care.* Deerfield Beach, FL: HCI Inc., 2002.

Byran, J., ed. *Love Is Ageless: Stories About Alzheimer's Disease,* second ed. Felton, CA: Lampico Creek Press, 2002.

Carroll, D. *When Your Loved One Has Alzheimer's Disease: A Caregiver's Guide.* New York: Harper and Row, 1989.

Caulking, M. *Design for Dementia.* Owings Mills, MD: National Health Publishing, 1998.

Dipple, R., and J. Hutton, eds. *Caring for the Alzheimer's Patient: A Practical Guide*. Buffalo: Prometheus Books, 1991.

Fitzray, B. J. *Alzheimer's Activities: Hundreds of Activities for Men and Women with Alzheimer's Disease and Related Disorders*. Windsor, CA: Rayve Productions, 2001.

Grey-Davidson, F. *The Alzheimer's Sourcebook for Caregivers: A Practical Guide for Getting Through the Day*. 2nd ed. New York: Macmillan, 1981.

Gwether, L. *Care of Alzheimer's Patients: A Manual for Nursing Home Staff*. Chicago: ADRDA, 1985.

Halry, W. "The Family Caregiver's Role in Alzheimer's Disease." *Neurology* 48 (1998): S225–S228.

Khachaturian, Z. "The Five-Ten, Ten-Ten Plan for Alzheimer's Disease." Editorial. *Neurobiology Aging* 13 (1992): 197–98.

Khalsa, D., and C. Ztauth. *Brain Longevity: The Breakthrough Program That Improves Your Mind and Memory*. New York: Warner Books, 1997.

Lawlor, B., ed. *Behavioral Complications in Alzheimer's Disease*. Washington: American Psychiatric Press, 1995.

Lipowski, Z. *Delirium: Acute Confusional States*. 2nd ed. New York: Oxford University Press, 1900.

Mace, N., and P. Rabin. *The 36-Hour Day: A Family Guide to Caring for the Person with Alzheimer's Disease, Related Dementing Illnesses, and Memory Loss in Later Life*. Baltimore: Johns Hopkins University Press, 1981.

Mendez, M., K. Underwood, A. Mastri, J. Sung, and W. Frey. "Risk Factors in Alzheimer's Disease: A Clinicopathologic Study." *Neurology* 42 (1998): 770–75.

Mittleman, M. S., C. Epstein, and A. Peirzchala. *Counseling the Alzheimer's Caregiver*. Chicago, IL: AMA Press, 2003.

Shenk, D. *The Forgetting: Alzheimer's: Portrait of an Epidemic.* New York: Doubleday, 2001.

Sheridan, C. *Failure-Free Activities for the Alzheimer's Patient.* Oakland, CA: Cottage Books, 1987.

Sogyal, R. *The Tibetan Book of Living and Dying.* New York: Harper, 1993.

Strauss, C. J. *Talking to Alzheimer's: Simple Ways to Connect When You Visit with a Family Member.* Oakland, CA: New Harbinger Publications, 2001.

White, L., and B. Spencer. *Moving a Relative with Memory Loss.* Santa Rosa, CA: Whisp Publications, 2000.

Zogola, J. *Doing Things: A Guide to Programming Activities for Persons with Alzheimer's Disease and Related Disorders.* Baltimore: Johns Hopkins University Press, 1997.

Resources

Internet Sources

- Alzforum: Alzheimer Research Forum—www.alzforum.org
- The Alzheimer's Disease Education and Referral Center—www.alzheimers.org
- The Alzheimer's Store—www.alzstore.com
- ALZwell Caregiver Page—www.alzwell.com
- Cognitive Care—www.cognitivecare.com
- Dementia.com—www.dementia.com
- ElderHope—www.elderhope.com
- MedWebPlus—www.medwebplus.com
- Memory Clinic—www.memoryclinic.com
- National Institute of Neurological Disorders and Stroke—www.ninds.nih.gov

Organizations

■ **Alzheimer's Association**
225 North Michigan Avenue
Chicago, IL 60601
(800) 272-3900

Each major city also has a local branch.

■ **National Council on the Aging**
(800) 424-9046

Can provide referrals to nearest adult care centers.

■ **American Health Assistance Foundation**
(800) 437-2423

Can provide educational material on Alzheimer's disease for caregivers.

Community Resources

Many community resources are available to caregivers of people with Alzheimer's. Contact your local Alzheimer's association or health department for information regarding support groups, physicians, respite care, and any other needs you may have.

Index